Thomas Hunter Weir

A Short History of the Hebrew Text of the Old Testament

Thomas Hunter Weir

A Short History of the Hebrew Text of the Old Testament

ISBN/EAN: 9783337417154

Printed in Europe, USA, Canada, Australia, Japan

Cover: Foto ©Lupo / pixelio.de

More available books at **www.hansebooks.com**

A SHORT HISTORY

OF

THE HEBREW TEXT

OF THE

OLD TESTAMENT

BY

THOMAS H. WEIR, B.D.

ASSISTANT TO PROFESSOR OF ORIENTAL LANGUAGES IN THE UNIVERSITY
OF GLASGOW.

WILLIAMS AND NORGATE,
14, HENRIETTA STREET, COVENT GARDEN, LONDON;
20, SOUTH FREDERICK STREET, EDINBURGH;
AND 7, BROAD STREET, OXFORD.
1899.

PREFACE.

The following pages would not have seen the light but for the fact that there is no precisely similar composition, going over the same ground, in existence. The object aimed at has been to trace the growth of the Hebrew text from its beginning until it reaches the form in which it appears to the reader of a modern printed Hebrew Bible. It has been sought to explain everything which meets the eye on the printed page, or to indicate where such explanation may be readily found.

In putting these pages together, I have especially to acknowledge my indebtedness to the Rev. Professor James Robertson, D.D. not only for indicating where the best sources of information on the various points were to be obtained, but also for carefully revising the proof-sheets; and also to the Rev. Professor Dickson,

LL.D., for reading a proof and suggesting many improvements.

The works which have been most freely used are Canon Taylor's *The Alphabet,* the introduction to Canon Driver's *Notes on the Hebrew Text of the Books of Samuel,* Dr. Ludwig Blau's *Masoretische Untersuchungen* and *Zur Einleitung in die heilige Schrift,* and, for the last chapter, Dr. Ginsburg's *Introduction to the Hebrew Bible.*

In regard to the plates, that of the Codex Babylonicus (p. 128) has been executed by Mr. James Hyatt, London; and that of the Carpentras Stele (p. 15) at the Clarendon Press, Oxford, with the permission of the authorities of the British Museum and of the Delegates of the Press. I have to express my indebtedness to the Rev. Canon Taylor for kindly offering, and to his publishers, Messrs. Kegan Paul, Trench, Trübner and Company, for consenting, to lend the *clichés* for the Baal Lebanon Inscription and Turin Papyrus (p. 7). The electros for the Hebrew Manuscript, British Museum, Oriental 4445 (p. 126), for the Siloam Inscription (p. 9) and for the set of Jewish Coins were supplied by Messrs. Wm. Collins, Sons and Company, Glasgow; and those of the Tell el Hesy Tablet (p. 4) by the Palestine Exploration Fund.

The History of the Hebrew Text of the Old Testament is an extremely interesting one. The following pages give only the barest outline. Perhaps the subject will be taken up and dealt with as it deserves by more capable hands.

Glasgow, 1899.

T. H. W.

CONTENTS.

                                                                Pages
Notes on the Plates   XI

CHAPTER I.
EARLIEST FORM OF WRITING IN ISRAEL.
1. Invention of Alphabetic Writing. 2. Before the Settlement in Canaan. 3. References to Writing in the Old Testament. 4. Inscriptions dated after the Settlement in Canaan. 5. Orthography of the Period . . . . 1—11

CHAPTER II.
THE TWO HEBREW SCRIPTS.
1. The Old Hebrew Alphabet. 2. Aramæan Scripts. 3. Orthography of the Period. 4. The New Hebrew Character. 5. Inscriptions in New Hebrew Character. 6. Summary. 7. Writing Materials . . . . 11—22

CHAPTER III.
THE CHANGE OF SCRIPT.
1. Various Theories. 2. The Change in the Law. 3. In the Other Books. 4. Evidence of Lxx. 5. Evidence of Text Itself. 6. Conclusion . . . . 23—34

CHAPTER IV.
THE PRESERVATION OF THE TEXT.
1. Internal Conditions. 2. External Circumstances. 3. The Lxx Version . . . . 34—41

CONTENTS.

CHAPTER V.
DESCRIPTION OF TEXT OF FIRST CENTURY.

1. Purely Consonantal. 2. Word-Separation. 3. Other Breaks in the Text. 4. The Final Forms of Letters. 5. Origin of Final Letters. 6. Talmudic Reference to Final Letters. 7. Conclusion. 8. The Vowel-Letters. 9. Anomalous Forms. 10. The Dotted Words. 11. Their Antiquity. 12. List of Passages. 13. The Inverted *Nuns*. 14. Large and Small Letters. 15. Suspended Letters and Divided *Nun*. 16. Abbreviations. 17. Summary . . . . 41—71

CHAPTER VI.
ALTERATION OF ORIGINAL DOCUMENTS.

A. Intentional Alteration. 1. יהוה and בעל 2. Euphemistic Expressions. 3. The Tiqqûn Soferim or 'Correction of the Scribes.' 4. The 'Iṭṭûr Soferim. B. Unintentional Alteration of Original Documents: Classification of Scribal Errors. 1. Failures to understand the Sense. 2. Errors due to the Eye. 3. Errors due to the Ear. 4. Failure of Memory. 5. Errors due to Carelessness or Ignorance. 6. Conclusion . . . . 71—88

CHAPTER VII.
PROGRESS OF HISTORY OF TEXT DURING FIRST SEVEN CHRISTIAN CENTURIES.

1. All Study of the Text was Oral. 2. The Text not always Read as Written. 3. Means to Preserve the Text . . 88—93

CHAPTER VIII.
DIVISION OF TEXT.

1. Verses. 2. Sections of the Law. 3. The Haftârahs. 4. The Poetical Books and Passages. 5. Number, Order and Names of the Books . . . . 93—100

CHAPTER IX.
THE VOCALIZATION OF THE TEXT.

1. The Antiquity of the Points. 2. The Upper Limit. 3. The Lower Limit. 4. The Probable Date. 5. Various Systems. 6. Various Recensions . . . . 101—108

CHAPTER X.
THE PALESTINIAN SYSTEM.

1. The Living Language. 2. The Consonants. 3. Dagesh Forte. 4. The Vowels. 5. Summary. 6. The Accents. 7. Peculiar Pointings . . . . 108—119

CHAPTER XI.
THE MASSORAH.

1. Definition of the Term. 2. The Qrîs and Sevîrs. 3. Other Parts of the Massorah . . . . 119—126

CHAPTER XII.
MANUSCRIPTS AND PRINTED TEXTS.

1. Manuscripts. 2. Printed Editions. 3. The Chapters. 4. Clausulæ Massoreticæ . . . . 126—141

Index of Scripture Texts 143

NOTES ON THE PLATES.

THE MOABITE STONE.

The following are the transliteration and translation of the first six lines. The dotted letters are doubtful.

אנך משע. בן. כמשגד. מלך. מאב הד
יבני‎|‎אבי. מלך. על. מאב. שלשן. שת ואנך. מלך
תי. אחר. אבי‎|‎ואעש. הבמת. זאת. לכמש. בקרחה.‎|‎ב
שע. כי. השעני. מכל. המלכן. וכי. הראני. בכל. שנאין עמׄ
י. מלך. ישראל. ויענו. את. מאב. ימן. רבן. כי. תאנף. כמש. בא
צה‎|‎ויחלפה. בנה. ויאמר. גם. הא. אענו. את. מאב‎|‎בימי. אמר.

I am Mesha the son of Chemoshgad king of Moab, the Dibonite. My father was king over Moab thirty years, and I reigned after my father. And I made this high-place to Chemosh in Q-r-ḥ-h . . . . . . because he saved me from all the kings, and because he made me to look upon all those that hated me. Omri was king of Israel, and he had afflicted Moab many days, for Chemosh was angry [fem.] with his land. And his son succeded him, and he also said, I will afflict Moab in my days. He said . . . . .

THE BAAL LEBANON INSCRIPTION AND TURIN PAPYRUS.

The translation of the former is given in the text: the following translation of the latter by Lenormant is offered in Canon Taylor's *Alphabet*;—

Deus, Domine mi, ex conculcatione servum tuum Pakhim e[ripe]

Vita unica et verax dominus meus Jehovah ....

THE SILOAM INSCRIPTION.

The lines in modern square Hebrew run as follows;—

(הן) הנקבה . וזה . היה . דבר . הנקבה . בעוד . . . . . .

הגרזן . אש . אל . רעו . ובעוד . שלש . אמת . לה . . . . קל . אש . ק

רא . אל . רעו . כי . הית . זדה . בצר . מימן . . . . וביםֿ . ה

נקבה . הכו . החצבם . אש . לקרת . רעו . גרזן . על . גרזן וילכו

המים . מן . המוצא . אל . הברכה . במאתים . ואלף . אמה . ומ . . .

ה . אמה . היה . גבח . הצר . על . החצב . . . . .

THE CARPENTRAS STELE.

The following are the transliteration and translation given in Canon Driver's *Text of the Books of Samuel*, p. XVIII.

תמנחא זי אוסרי אלהא	בריכה תבא ברת תחפי
וכרצי איש לא אמרת תמה	מנדעם באיש לא עבדת
מן קדם אוסרי מן קחי	קדם אוסרי בריכה הוי
ובין חסיה	הוי פלחה נמעתי

Blessed be Taba, the daughter of Taḥapi, devoted worshipper of the God Osiris. Aught of evil she did not, and calumny against any man she never uttered. Before Osiris be thou blessed: from Osiris take thou water. Be thou a worshipper (sc. before Osiris), my darling; and among the pious [mayest thou be at peace!]

PALMYRENE AND HEBREW INSCRIPTIONS.

a. This inscription is in the uncial Palmyrene character and does not show the ligatures; but these very much resemble those in the Hebrew (no. 6). The transliteration is;—

לבעל שמן מרא עלמן קרב
כפתא וערשא אגתנגלס

that is;—"To Baal of heaven, lord of the worlds, has offered the canopy *and* couch Agathangelus."

The inscription is from Reland's *Palæstina*.

Nos. 1, 2 and 2a are referred to in the text p. 18. They are taken from Chwolson's *Corp. Inscr. Hebr.*

6 and 17. The transliteration and translation are;—

זה . . . . ב . לאלעזר חניה יועזר יהודה . . . . . יוחנן
בני יוסף . . . . . . סף ואלעזר בני חניה
. . . . . . בני חזיר

"This [is the grave] of Eleazar, Hanniah, Joezer, Judah . . . . Johanan, sons of Joseph . . . . seph and Eleazar, sons of Hanniah . . . . sons of Hezir."

יהי שלום במקום הזה ובכל מקומות ישראל יוסה הלוי בן לוי
עשה השקוף הזה תבא ברכה במעשיו [במעיוש]

"Peace be upon this place and upon all the places of Israel. Joseh the Levite, son of Levi, made this lintel: may blessing come upon his works."

XIV NOTES ON THE PLATES.

One might say that, even if it were not known independently, one would be safe in inferring the monotheism of the Jews from the inartistic character of their inscriptions.

JEWISH COINS.

The silver shekel of Simon the Maccabee has, on the obverse the legend שקל ישראל, *Shekel of Israel* and the date א, that is the first year of independence, or 142 B.C.: on the reverse, ירושלים הקדושה, *Jerusalem the Holy*. The chalice is thought to represent the pot of manna: the triple lily or hyacinth, Aaron's rod. Many refer these coins to the years 66—70 A.D.

The design of the half-shekel is the same as that of the shekel, except that instead of *Shekel of Israel* there stand the words חצי השקל, *The half-shekel*.

THE SUPERLINEAR PUNCTUATION.

In the ordinary or Palestinian system of vocalization, the passage is pointed thus;—

וְיִסְקוּן יָתַהּ בְּנֵי אַהֲרֹן לְמַדְבְּחָא עַל עֲלָתָא דִי עַל אָעַיָא דִי עַל אֶשָׁתָא קָרְבַּן דְמִתְקַבַּל בְּרַעֲוָא קֳדָם יְיָ: etc.

The pointing kindly supplied by Dr. Chamizer should be compared with the specimen given in Baer's *Job;* and also with that of Merx' *Chrestomathia Targumica.*

THE RABBINIC BIBLE.

This page is from the Warsaw edition of 1862. It shows, in the first place a poetical passage of the text arranged like the bricks in a wall. The column on the left is the Targum, which, being longer than the text, extends also below it. Between the two columns is the massorah parva, and immediately beneath the targum, the massorah magna. These are surrounded by three commentaries: to the top and right, that of Rashi, i. e. Rabbi Solomon ben Isaac; to the top and left, that of Radaq, i. e. Rabbi David Kimchi; and along the bottom that of Ralbag, i. e. Rabbi Levi ben Gerson. At the foot of the page are two late hagadic commentaries.

CHAPTER I.

EARLIEST FORM OF WRITING IN ISRAEL.

1. *Invention of Alphabetic Writing.* At what period of their history the Israelites became acquainted with the art of writing is uncertain. In their traditional history as given in the Old Testament, the art is not referred to before the time of Moses. In the whole of the book of Genesis there is no mention of writing and the verb meaning to write does not once occur. In the account of the acquisition by Abraham of the cave of Machpelah given in the twenty-third chapter of Genesis, nothing is said of a written document or bill of purchase, such as we read of in the similar transaction recorded in the thirty-second chapter of Jeremiah. Mention is made, indeed, in the thirty-eighth chapter of Genesis, of a signet-ring, but this does not necessarily imply an engraved inscription.

As to the period at which alphabetic writing began to be used, the commonly accepted view is that about the year 1500 B.C. it was pretty generally practised among the Phœnicians. It is not, however, likely, in the nature of things, that the Israelites were in their nomadic state acquainted with alphabetic writing. More probably they acquired the art at the time of their settlement on the East and West of the Jordan.

The form of writing in use in Palestine about the year 1400 B.C., at least for purposes of international correspondence, was the syllabic Babylonian cuneiform. The Hebrews, however, do not appear ever to have adopted this: at any rate, they are not known ever to have employed a script other than alphabetic.

Both the Greek and the Hebrew alphabets go back to the same original. This original script was purely alphabetic and it had a Semitic origin, that is to say, its inventors spoke a Semitic language whether they were themselves Semites or not. The Classical authors are unanimous in their assertion that the Greeks received the alphabet from the Phœnicians (Herod. v, 58); but as to the original inventors of the alphabet, they variously assign that honour to the Phœnicians (Lucan, Pharsalia iii, 220), Syrians, Assyrians or Egyptians (Tacitus, Annals xi, 14: Pliny, Nat. Hist. ed. Sillig, vii, 192). The opinion now generally held is that the Phœnicians found alphabetic signs in use in Egypt and adopted these to the exclusion of all others somewhere about the year 1900 B.C. Such a great simplification in the process of writing would naturally appeal to a commercial people such as they were. That the alphabet is the invention of a Semitic people is proved by the fact of guttural letters which are peculiar to the Semitic languages being represented in it, as well as by the absence of letters to indicate vowel sounds. At the same time, the possession of an alphabet does not exclude the simultaneous employment of a less developed form of writing.

2. *Before the Settlement in Canaan.* Of the literature and script which existed in Canaan immediately before the immigration of the Israelites some remains have come down to us in the Tell el Amarna tablets. These number about three hundred, and were discovered in 1887 by a peasant woman at Tell el Amarna in Upper Egypt, the site of the ancient Arsinoe on the east bank of the Nile. They consist for the most part of letters sent by the vassal kings of the Amorites, Philistines and Phœnicians, to Egypt to Amenophis IV, one of the kings of the XVIIIth dynasty, whose capital Arsinoe was. They are written in the Aramaic language and in the cuneiform, that is, a non-alphabetic script, and belong to the fourteenth or fifteenth century B. C.

On the 14th May 1892 there was discovered at Tell el Hesy, the site of the Lachish of the Old Testament, a precisely similar tablet. This forms the only pre-

Israelitish inscription as yet found in Palestine. It was discovered in the Amorite stratum of the mound, and mentions Zimridi, who was king of Lachish about the year 1400 B. C. and who is also mentioned on the tablets found in Egypt. English versions of this interesting and solitary relic will be found in Lieut.-Colonel Conder's book on the Tell el Amarna Tablets, and in the Quarterly Statement of the Palestine Exploration Fund for Jan. 1893 by Professor Sayce. The translations, however, do not agree.

If the Israelites ever acquired and employed this script, which they found in use in the country of their adoption, no remains of it have come down to our time from them.

3. *References to Writing in the Old Testament.* The earliest reference to writing to be found in the Old Testament is Ex. 17, 14, where Moses is commanded to write in a book an account of the victory just gained over Amalek in Rephidim, and this may have been the first entry in the Book of the Wars of Jehovah mentioned in Num. 21, 14. In Ex. 24, 7 Moses reads the Book of the Covenant, that is, Exodus 20—23 inclusive, in the audience of the people and thereafter goes up into the Mountain to receive the two tables of the Law. From this point onwards, the references to

THE TELL EL HESY TABLET.

writing occur with increasing frequency, but it is to be noted that it is always as a means of storing up and preserving what is written, not of circulating it. The art of writing is a possession of the few and the diffusion or publication of literature takes place orally. But when we come down to the times of the Judges, the fact that a chance prisoner was able to write down the princes of Succoth for Gideon (Jud. 8, 14), seems to point to the knowledge of reading and writing being general.

In view, however, of the late date now assigned to most of the earlier books of the Old Testament, it is maintained that statements such as these are valid only for the period in which the author wrote, not for that of which he treated.

Yet the word which came later to signify 'scribe' is found in the Song of Deborah (Jud. 5, 14, A. V.):

Out of Machir came down governors,
And out of Zebulon they that handle the pen of the writer,

and this poem is generally admitted to be the composition of a poet who was contemporary with the events which he describes. The word translated *pen*, however, properly means *staff* and that for *scribe* may in this passage mean no more than *chief*, the poet wishing to give variety to his vocabulary.

By the beginning of the monarchy, in any case, it

is evident that the higher officials at court must have possessed a knowledge of writing as well as the king (2 Sam. 11, 14) and the nobles (8, 17); and yet reading remained so long an accomplishment of the few, that even as late as the reigns of Ahab and Joash, we find that Elijah and Elisha do not as a rule think it worth while to put their discourses in writing. Samuel, indeed, reduced to writing the constitution of the new Israelitish monarchy (1 Sam. 10, 25), and written laws existed before the time of the earliest writing prophets (Hos. 8, 12); but of written literature in the strict sense there appears at this period to have been none. Only laws were written and annals: the rest was diffused and handed down orally. Yet so great a change had come over the people within the next hundred years, that not only do Amos and Hosea write their discourses, but it is by many supposed that the old sacred legends of the Patriarchs, of the Judges and of David, which had until now been passed on from one generation to another by word of mouth, were now for the first time made permanent in writing. Similarly the poetry of the Arabs of the Time of Ignorance, and even that composed after the coming of Muhammed, were not written down until the close of the first century A. H. Even Jeremiah, like many a famous Arabian poet or like the 'illiterate Prophet'

[To face p. 7]

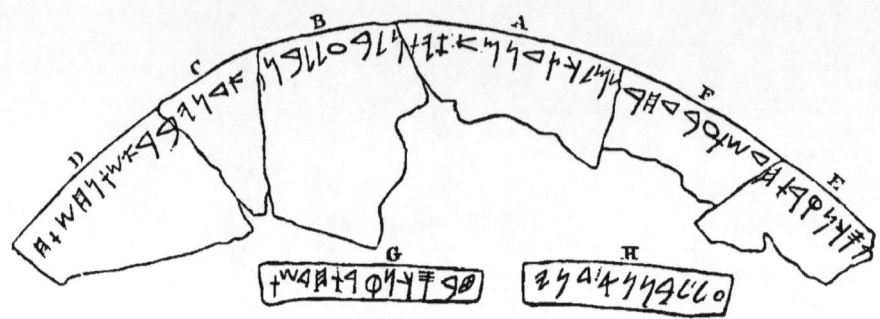

סכן קרת חדשת עבד חרם מלך צדנם אז יתן לבעל לבנן
אדני בראשת נחשת ח

THE BAAL LEBANON INSCRIPTION.

אל מראי מתדוהשת עבדך פחים ש...
היא חדה ושרירא מראי יהוי יק...

THE TURIN PAPYRUS (*Egyptian Aramaic, p. 15*).

himself, does not seem to have written anything, whether he could have done so or not.

In order to determine in what script the earlier prophets, Amos, Hosea, Micah and Isaiah and their contemporaries wrote, it is necessary to turn to the inscriptions which have survived and have been discovered up to the present time.

4. *Inscriptions dated after the Settlement in Canaan.* The script which prevailed during this period, not only in Palestine itself but also in the countries bordering upon it, was the Phœnician. The following are the principal inscriptions:—

1. The most ancient specimen of the Phœnician script extant is the inscription of Baal Lebanon. It is made up of eight fragments of bronze and was found near the summit of a mountain in Cyprus some twenty miles from Limasol. Six of these form consecutive portions of the rim of a bowl about one foot in diameter and the inscription on them runs: "This vessel of bronze was offered by a citizen of Carthage, servant of Hiram, king of the Sidonians, to Baal Lebanon his Lord." The two remaining portions are detached. The bowl is supposed to have formed part of the plunder of a temple on the Lebanon which had been carried to Cyprus. The forms of the letters are the most ancient known and are assigned to the

beginning of the ninth century. The Carthage mentioned is not the African city: the name means New Town and might well be common.

2. By far the longest and most important Phœnician inscription of this period yet discovered is the well-known Moabite Stone, which was found at Dhibân, the ancient Dibon, in 1868 and which is now in the Louvre. This stele measured forty-one inches by twenty-one and the inscription ran to thirty-four lines. The author of the inscription is Mesha, the king of Moab who is referred to in 2 Kings 1, 1 and chap. 3. In it he relates how he threw off the yoke of the king of Israel, recovered and rebuilt his towns—most of which are mentioned in Is. 15 and 16 and Jer. 48—constructed a road across the Arnon and subsequently undertook an expedition against the Edomites. The date of the inscription is about the year 896 in the ordinary chronology. The letters present the appearance of having been drawn by a scribe and cut by an illiterate mason. The genuineness of the stone has not been unquestioned.

3. The fifteen lion-weights—weights in the form of a lion—discovered at Nineveh, for the most part bear legends in both cuneiform and Phœnician characters. They belong to the latter part of the eighth and the beginning of the seventh century. Other small

[To face p. 9]

THE SILOAM INSCRIPTION.
(From a Squeeze.)
TRANSLATION.

1st Line, "{Behold} the excavation! Now this had been the history of the excavation. While the workmen were still lifting up
2nd "   the axe, each towards his neighbour, and while three cubits still remained to (cut through), (each heard) the voice of
          the other who called to his neighbour, since there was an excess in the rock on the right hand and on (the left). And on the day of the
3rd "   excavation the workmen struck, each to meet his neighbour, axe against axe, and there flowed
4th "   excavation from the spring to the pool for a thousand and two hundred cubits; and . . . .
5th "   the waters from the spring to the pool over the heads of the workmen.
6th "   of a cubit was the height of the rock over the heads of the workmen.
                                                    [2 Kings xx. 20. 2 Chron. xxxii. 30.]

remains in the same character have been found elsewhere.

4. But not only was the Phœnician alphabet known and in general use in the countries bordering upon Palestine: it was the form of writing employed by the Israelites themselves during the period under review. This fact, which had been long recognised on other grounds, has been put beyond question by the discovery in the year 1880 of the Siloam Inscription. An account of this 'find' may be read in the Quarterly Statements of the Palestine Exploration Fund for the year 1881. This inscription is engraved on a recessed tablet in the wall of the tunnel connecting the pool of Siloam with St. Mary's well. The letters are over half-an-inch in height, deeply incised. The language is pure Hebrew and the script similar to that of the Moabite Stone, but exhibiting a later phase. It is not earlier than the eighth nor later than the sixth century. Most likely it belongs to the reign of Hezekiah, the tunnel being the conduit referred to as being the work of Hezekiah in 2 K. 20, 20: 2 Chr. 32, 30: Ecclus. 48, 17. Or, the tunnel may be the work of an earlier time, in which case 'the waters of Shiloah that go softly', spoken of by Isaiah (8, 6), would mean the waters flowing through the Siloam tunnel.

The Siloam Inscription shows the alphabet in use

in ancient Israel to be a form of Phœnician not materially different from the other early examples extant. Some of the letters betray a slight movement towards a more advanced type: others, such as the ח with three bars and the triangular ע, show a more archaic form. The long tails are due solely to the taste and fancy of the artist.

5. *Orthography of the Period.* 1. Word-separation: Both on the Moabite Stone and on the Siloam Inscription the words are separated by a point, as in the oldest Greek inscriptions.

2. Vowel-letters: The *scriptio plena* is rare. The Moabite Stone regularly omits the י of the plural and dual. In the Siloam Inscription יום, קול, חוצבים, ימין, צור, אמות and איש are all written defectively, but מוצא, עוד and ראש in full. For the last the Moabite Stone has רש and it even omits to indicate final vowels as in אנכי=אנך. The suffixal י and the verbal affix תי are, however, fully written. The suffix of the 3rd pers. sing. masc. is indicated by the letter ה in the Moabite Stone but by ו in the Siloam Inscription, which even writes רעו where the Old Testament Text would have רעהו.

3. Except the word-divider there are no vowel or other points.

4. There are no special forms of letters when final as ץ ף ן ם ך.

5. There is no hesitation about dividing words at the ends of lines, even in the middle of a syllable.

6. The writing is from right to left.

7. The letter ס does not occur.

CHAPTER II.

THE TWO HEBREW SCRIPTS.

1. *The Old Hebrew Alphabet.* The old Hebrew alphabet, like the Phœnician, consisted of twenty-two letters, all consonants.

The ORDER in which the letters followed one another is known first of all from the order of the letters of the Greek alphabet taken according to their numerical values. This is confirmed, though not perhaps till the time of the Exile, by the alphabetic Psalms and by the figure called *athbash*, אתבש. Examples of the latter are found in the Bible in Jer. 25, 26 and 51, 1 and 41. In this cipher a word is disguised by substituting the last letter of the alphabet for the first, the second last for the second and so on. Hence the name. Thus in the passages cited בבל is called ששך and כשדים becomes לב קמי, which the Authorized Version translates: 'In the midst of them that rise up against me'. Later or, it may be, earlier, there are the acrostic Psalms 9 and 10, 25, 34, 37, 111, 112, 119 and 145. The other alphabetic portions of the Old Testament are Lam. 1—4: Pr. 31, 10—31 and possibly the beginning of Nahum. In all these the order of the letters is the same as that to which we are accustomed, with one or two exceptions. Thus there seems to be some doubt as to the place of the letter פ. In Lam. 2—4 it precedes ע. In Ps. 37 the ע is obscured. Pss. 25 and 34, apparently both the work of the same author, omit ו and append a second verse commencing with פ at the conclusion. These and other anomalies, however, may be nothing more than corruptions of the text or they may be due to a preference of the sense to the form on the part of the poet. The originality of the present order appears also from this, that the letters standing together bear similar names, as י and כ (hand), מ (water) and נ (fish), ק and ר (head). In the case of the Ethiopic the halves of the alphabet were transposed, whence the conjectural etymology of the word *element*=LMN=ABC.

The NAMES of the letters are supposed to have been applied to them from a fancied resemblance of the Egyptian signs to certain objects. In this case we must assume that these had ceased to bear any very striking resemblance to their original, so that, what had once been the picture of a foot the Phœnicians took for a house, and in what had once been a reed they recognised an ox. In any case the names of the letters are extremely ancient, being the same in Hebrew, Greek and, with exceptions, Ethiopic; and the fact that the Hebrew names are not Hebrew vocables makes it the more probable that they are original. The names are given on the acrophonic principle, each beginning with the letter of which it is the name. Thus in Ethiopic the word for Hand does not begin with y, and so the letter ׳ is called *yaman*, right hand. Similarly, the word *nun*, 'fish', being obsolete, the letter נ is called *naḥash* serpent. In Arabic the names are cut down to monosyllables. The Hebrew names are given for the first time in the LXX version of Lam. 1—4. The Greek names Alpha, Beta and so on are either feminine or emphatic masculine forms of the Hebrew. In Gamma=galma=gamla or in Sigma=simka there is also a transposition of letters.

In passing over from the Phœnicians to the Greeks the alphabet necessarily underwent various modifications. The letters representing the four guttural sounds which are peculiar to the Semitic languages lost their consonantal value altogether and became vowels, that is ק ה ח ע became AEHO, the letters being inverted with the change in the direction of the writing. The peculiar Semitic guttural *qoph* was rejected in Greek as a letter, but retained as a numerical sign for 90 under its old name. It has survived as a letter in the Latin Q. *Vav* is only a numeral in Greek, with its Hebrew value of 6, but is the Latin F. *Samekh* gave its place, form and numerical value of 60 to the Greek Ξ, but its name to the Greek Σ which has the place and form of *sin*. Tsadhe is dropped as a letter, but appears as the numeral *sampi*=900, the present value of the modern final ϟ.

But whilst the Greek alphabet retained the forms and even the names of the old Hebrew or Phœnician letters almost without alteration, the Eastern scripts diverged more and more from them. The destruction of Phœnician trade by the later Assyrian kings, and especially the conquest of Tyre by Nebuchadnezzar about the year 572, led to the decay and almost complete disappearance of the Phœnician script from south-western Asia, and to the substitution in its place, for purposes of commerce and international intercourse, of the Aramean.[1]

2. *Aramean Scripts.* The oldest specimens of the

---

[1] Charts showing how one language supplanted another in western Asia will be found in Hommel's Die Semiten und ihre Bedeutung für die Kulturgeschichte.

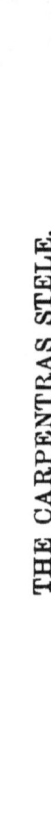

THE CARPENTRAS STELE.

Aramean alphabet which have survived are a few characters inscribed on the cuneiform clay tablets of Nineveh, as the Phœnician letters were upon the lion-weights. They belong to the seventh century. Later this script is found on the coins of the numerous Persian Satraps down to the time of Alexander the Great, 333 B.C. There is very little noticeable in the way of divergence from the Phœnician during this period beyond the opening of the loops of certain letters such as B and D; ら and ⊿ become ⊔ and ㄐ.

2. Meantime an Aramean script is found in Egypt. The oldest instance of its occurrence is the stele of Saqqārah near Cairo found in 1877. It belongs to the year 482 B.C., but the letters are indistinct; and the cardinal example of the Egyptian Aramaic is the memorial tablet called, after the French town where it now lies, the Carpentras Inscription, belonging to the latter part of the fourth century. There are also a number of papyri which bring the history of this script down to the first century B.C., several being compositions of a religious nature apparently by Jews.[1]

3. A third stage in the development of the Aramean alphabet is found in the series of inscriptions belonging

---

[1] Oriental Series of Palæographical Soc. plates 25, 26 and 63.

to the first three Christian centuries and known as the Palmyrene. One of these and probably the oldest is dated the year 9 B. C. Several have been found in Algeria and one as far north as South Shields; but by far the greater number have been found at Palmyra and belong to the time of Odenathus and Zenobia, 266—273 A. D. Hence the name. There are two varieties of this script, a highly ornate uncial and a cursive. The language in which the inscriptions are written is a dialect of Aramaic resembling the Biblical.

3. *Orthography of the Period.* 1. Word-separation: The words are no longer divided by a point as in the Moabite Stone and Siloam Inscription but (except in the Palmyrene) by a space.

2. Vowel letters are used as freely as in the present text of the Old Testament.

3. There is still no trace of vowel or other points.

4. The use of ligatures in the Egyptian Aramaic and in the Palmyrene involved a distinction of initial and final forms of letters so connected. In some of the Egyptian papyri the letters *kaph, lamed* and *nun* have each two forms.

5. The most important point to note at present is that the Aramean scripts diverge from the Phœnician in the direction of the Hebrew square character, until in the Palmyrene they become almost identical with

it. This is seen most distinctly (a) in the opening of the loops of the letters *beth, daleth, ṭeth, qoph* and *resh:* 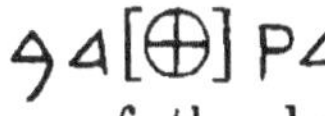 become 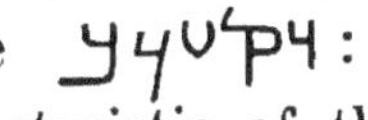: (b) in the omission of the bars characteristic of the letters *he, vav, zayin, ḥeth* and *tau*; and (c) in the tails of the *kaph, lamed, mem, pe* and *tsadhe,* which are vertical in the old Aramaic, beginning in the Egyptian Aramaic to curve towards the left.

4. *The New Hebrew Character.* After the return of the Jewish exiles from Babylon the Phœnician script had ceased to be the channel of commercial intercourse in the countries bordering upon Palestine. It had passed on to the West and its place had been taken by the more cursive Aramaic in Mesopotamia, Cilicia and Syria, and in Egypt where it was the script employed by the Jews in the second century before Christ, if not earlier still. At the same time the Aramaic Language became the *lingua franca* of the Seleucid Empire displacing Assyrian, Babylonian, Hebrew and Phœnician. In Syria the Aramean script divided into two branches: a northern which grew into Syriac, and a southern or Jewish from which the Hebrew square character was produced, some time before the commencement of the Christian era.

5. *Inscriptions in New Hebrew Character.* The oldest example of the Hebrew square character is

thought to be an inscription found in a cave at Araq al Ameer near Heshbon which was used as a place of retreat in the year 176 B.C.[1] The inscription, which may date much later than that, consists of five letters, which are variously read עךביה, Arabhyah, and טוביה, Tobiah, according to the initial letter which is doubtful. In either case two of the letters belong to the old script: on the latter reading the *scriptio plena* is to be observed.

A number of other short inscriptions, all probably to be assigned to the century before the destruction of Jerusalem by Titus in the year 70 A.D., have been found. Two identical inscriptions[2] were found near the supposed site of ancient Gezer bearing the words תחם גזר, that is, Limit of Gezer. But the longest inscription of this period is that over the entrance of the so-called Tomb of St. James, really the tomb of the Bene Hezir mentioned in 1 Chr. 24, 15, Neh. 10, 21. The letters are in the square character but very rudely formed. The final *nun* is distinguishable from the medial, but not so *pe;* and *vav, zayin* and *yod* are scarcely to be distinguished from one another. Ligatures are used.[3]

---

[1] Josephus Ant. xii, 4, 11: Chwolson Corp. Inscr. Hebr. no. I: Driver p. XXII.
[2] Chwolson nos. II and II a.   [3] Driver p. XXIII.

[To face p. 18]

PALMYRENE (a) AND HEBREW INSCRIPTIONS.

(The numbers are those of Chwolson's Corp. Inscr. Hebr.)

1. Inscription of Araq al Ameer.
2 and 2 a. Inscriptions found near Gezer.
6. The Beni Hezir inscription.
17. Inscription from Kefr Birim.

The inscriptions of the next two centuries are found outside Palestine; but in the year 1863 Renan discovered among the ruins of one of the synagogues of Kefr Birim near Safed an inscription[1] which he assigned to about the year 300 A.D., though it may well be earlier. In it "the transition to the Hebrew square character may be said to be accomplished"[2]. The *scriptio plena* is regular, and final ם, ן and ף are used.

During the subsequent centuries inscriptions are found all over the then civilized world in Italy, France, Spain, at Babylon, Tiflis and Derbend. From Aden there are two dated inscriptions, one of the year 916 which is also the date of the oldest dated Hebrew Manuscript[3]. The forms of the letters in this latter are the same as those in use at the present day, but without the uniform squareness, the great resemblances between different letters, and the useless tags and apices added to the forms by way of ornament. These are due to a later and vicious style.

6. *Summary.* Thus the Hebrew square character as seen in the printed texts of the Old Testament is a development of a branch of the Aramean script, which was also the mother of the two other great

---

[1] Chwolson no. 17.   [2] Driver p. XXV.
[3] The dates of the Crimean tombstones and MSS are generally regarded as forgeries.

Semitic literary scripts, Arabic and Syriac. By the third century B.C. the Aramean script was in general use in those countries where Assyrian, Babylonian, Hebrew and Phœnician had been employed before. But though general, its use was not universal in southwestern Asia. To this day the Samaritan Bible—the five Books of Moses—is read from a form of the old Hebrew or Phœnician character; and in the time of the Maccabees, and even as late as the war of Bar Cochba 135 A. D., coins were struck in the same character as is found on the Moabite Stone, a thousand years earlier.

The question now arises: When, if ever, were the Jewish Scriptures transliterated from the old Hebrew of the Siloam Inscription, in which the more ancient portions were originally written down, into the square character of the present day? But before proceeding to this point it will be convenient here to say something about the writing materials employed by the Hebrews before and after the Exile.

7. *Writing materials.*[1] The stylus עט was made of a material suitable to the substance on which it was intended to be used. For engraving on stone or metal an iron style was used, Job 19, 24, sometimes furnished

---

[1] Benzinger, Hebräische Archæologie, p. 290.

with a diamond point, Jer. 17, 1. In one obscure passage, Is. 8, 1, the chisel חרט is mentioned as a writing instrument: it has probably some connection with the name given to the Egyptian sacred scribes חרטמים in Genesis, Exodus and, after them, in Daniel. Otherwise the style was such a reed as was used in Egypt from the earliest times. In Ps. 45, 2 the LXX rightly translate by κάλαμος.

The pen-knife mentioned in Jer. 36, 23 was used to sharpen the calamus.

The ink, Jer. 36, 18, was carried in the ink-horn, Ezek. 9, 2, as at the present day in the girdle of the professional scribe.

The oldest material used for writing upon was in Syria as in Babylon clay, as is proved by the Tell el Amarna tablets. Documents which it was desired to preserve were engraved on stone or metal. Probably גליון Is. 8, 1 means not a roll, as the Authorized Version has it, but such a metal tablet. The plural is translated 'glasses' at ch. 3, 23, that is, metal mirrors. Lead tablets were in use among the Greeks and Romans, but in Job 19, 24 the meaning seems to be tracing out the letters themselves in molten lead upon the rock. 2 Esdras 14, 24 mentions boxwood as one material used, cf. Luke 1, 63.

Such materials however were soon discarded for

ordinary use, and by the times of the kings we already read of 'books' being used, if not earlier, Ex. 24, 7: Is. 30, 8 and often. The papyrus plant, Is. 18, 2, extinct in Lower Egypt, still grows abundantly in Palestine in the Huleh, the plain of Gennesaret and elsewhere, and may have furnished the material of which books were made. Yet the Old Testament nowhere mentions paper as being used for that purpose: the word occurs 2 John 12, 2 Esdras 15, 2, Tobit 7, 14. Neither is there any evidence in the Old Testament for the use of skins, though the LXX have the words χαρτίον and χάρτης in Jer. 36 (in the Greek 43). The only scriptural passage where parchment is mentioned is 2 Tim. 4, 13, and Josephus speaks of a magnificent roll of the Law written on parchment as having been sent to Egypt in the year 285 B.C.

The books were in the form of rolls, Ezek. 2, 9, each end of which was wound round a staff. The writing was in columns, Jer. 36, 23, beginning from the right hand staff. Sometimes the roll was written on both sides.

CHAPTER III.

THE CHANGE OF SCRIPT.

1. *Various Theories.* As to the question of the change of script from the old Hebrew of the Siloam Inscription to the modern square character, the fact of any change at all having taken place has been denied. This was the opinion of Eleazar of Modin, †135 A.D., which he founded on a Rabbinic deduction from the mention of the hooks of the pillars in Ex. 27, 10, as well as on the mention of the Jewish script and language in Esther 8, 9: he said that the language had not changed and so the script had remained unchanged also.

Another opinion was that, though the script had changed, yet the square character was the original. The Patriarch Rabbi Jehuda the Holy, the collector of the Mishnah, b. 135, d. c. 210, who generally goes by the name of Rabbi without any further qualification, said: The Law was given to Israel in the square character: when they sinned the script was changed to רעץ; and when they repented in Ezra's time the old character was restored. He founds this opinion on Zech. 9, 12: 'Turn again to the stronghold ye prisoners of hope: even to-day do I declare that I will render double unto thee.' He says the stronghold is

Jerusalem and to render double, משנה, means to restore the law to its old garb. רעץ is supposed to be a mistake for דעץ and to be the *deession* of Epiphanius, the form of script used on monuments, that is, the Phœnician.

Neither of these opinions, however, is to be accepted; because they are not based on any tradition, but solely on exegetical and theological or hagadic grounds —on a conviction of the sanctity and immutability of even the form of the letter of Scripture.

The same view, however, as to the existence and use of the present Hebrew character by the Israelites before the Exile has been put forward within recent years, on another ground,—that the conservative mind of the post-exilic Jews makes any change of script after that event impossible[1]. But this assumption seems to be disposed of by the fact of the striking of coins in the old character so late as the second Christian century and at a moment of intense religious and national excitement.

By others[2] the injunction given to Isaiah (8, 1) to 'write with the pen of a man' is interpreted as meaning to write in a certain character, and it is always possible that one form of script may have been employed

---

[1] Strack.   [2] Hoffmann.

for writing on stone and another for metal tablets and parchment or papyrus, as in Egypt there were, according to Clemens Alexandrinus and Porphyry, three scripts in use at one and the same time, the Hieroglyphic, Hieratic and Demotic, though Herodotus mentions only two (ii, 36) a profane and a sacred. It is true, also, that the upper classes in Isaiah's time spoke both Hebrew and Aramaic, 2 K. 18, 26=Is. 36, 11, and could read the latter, 2 K. 5, 7, but it does not follow that they were in the habit of writing their own language with Aramaic letters, and the passage Is. 8, 1 probably only means to write distinctly in large letters, and not in the ordinary cursive hand. And there is no reason to doubt that the characters found on the Siloam Inscription are the characters in which Isaiah wrote the autographs of his prophecies, and in which all the pre-exilic literature of the Hebrews was written down.

In dealing with the question as to when the change of script took place, it is convenient to make a distinction between the Law and the rest of the books. In the case of the latest books no change would be necessary, if their authors already wrote in the square character.

2. *The Change in the Law.* The most ancient authority on the change of script of the Hebrew lawbooks is Eleazar ben Jacob who lived after the middle of the first century A.D. He states that *a prophet* at the time of the return from the Captivity declared that the Torah was to be written in the square character. The next authority is about a century later, when R. Jose states, after Ezra 4, 7, that Ezra introduced both a new script and a new language. But the *locus classicus* on this point is a passage in the Talmud, treatise Sanhedrin 21 b, where it is said: 'Originally the Law was given to Israel in the Hebrew character and in the holy tongue: it was given again to them in the days of Ezra in the Assyrian character and in the Aramaic tongue. Israel chose for herself the Assyrian character and the holy tongue and left the Hebrew character and the Aramaic tongue to the הדיוטות'. In this passage the old script is called Hebrew, כתב עברי: the modern square character כתב אשורי. There are three possible explanations of the term אשורי. The first is that it is equivalent to מאשר, i.e. straight, or as the script came to be named later, square, מרבע. Then there is the explanation of R. Levi of the third century that אשורי means Assyrian; and this term again is capable of two interpretations. It may be loosely used for Babylonian as it is in Num. 24, 22. 24: Herod. i, 106, 178; and so the Talmudic שעלו עמהם מאשור, 'which letters came up with them from Babylon;' or again אשורי may be loosely used for

Syrian, that is, Aramaic. Cf. the LXX rendering of Jer. 35 (42), 11 and their appendix to Job. The word הדיוטות was explained by R. Hasda † 309 as meaning the Cutheans, that is Samaritans, 2 K. 17, 24. But this explanation is due to malice, and the word is to be taken in its proper sense as the transliteration of the Greek ἰδιῶται the equivalent of the Hebrew עם הארץ, the uninstructed laity.

The Talmudic tradition from the second century onwards is unanimous in crediting Ezra with the introduction of the square character, as far as the Law was concerned. These statements cannot be accepted on their own merits; for until the second century there is no reference to Ezra, and the tradition of the first century only mentions an unnamed prophet of Ezra's time. Moreover, as has been frequently remarked, the Talmud is very prone to assign to Ezra everything which can by no possibility be referred to Moses. All that can be inferred from such statements is that, as is known already from Matt. 5, 18, in the first century the square character was employed in the copies of the Law. The foreign origin of this script was acknowledged, and regarded as an uncomfortable fact which had to be made the best of. Hence the change of script was either denied altogether, or represented as a reversion to the original usage or, lastly, the responsibility was laid on the shoulders of an acknowledged authority such as Ezra and so legalized. But the necessity for such a reference at all seems to point to the fact that the new script was still, in the first century, of disputed authority, although it had then been employed for such a length of time that its origin was lost. A further objection to Ezra as the originator of the new practice is the absence of any mention of such a thing in the books of Ezra and Nehemiah, whoever the author of these books may have been.

The testimony of Josephus points to an Aramaic script. In Antiquities xii, 2, 4 he makes Demetrius, the librarian of Ptolemy II, Philadelphus (284-247) speak of the Law as written in *Hebrew* characters; but in the first section of the same chapter he speaks of there being many books of laws among the Jews which were worthy of being added to the king's library but which, being written in a language and a character of their own, yet very like the Aramaic, would be difficult of translation.

The question is still further complicated by the existence among the Samaritans of a character very little removed from the old Hebrew. The Samaritans are a mixed race descended from the northern Israelites who remained in the land after the deportation of 722, and the foreign colonists then introduced, 2 K. 17, 24. On the return of the Jews from the Babylonian Captivity they offered their assistance in rebuilding the walls and temple of Jerusalem. This the Jews, who had been made more exclusive by exile, declined, refusing also to allow the Samaritans to participate in their worship. On Nehemiah's return to Jerusalem he found that they had succeeded in establishing themselves there and that the daughter of Sanballat had been married to the high priest's grandson (13, 28). Expelled by Nehemiah, this person seems to have removed with those Jews who refused to be ruled by Nehemiah, to Samaria, establishing there an organized religious community. These events occurred about the year 433, but Josephus thought they happened exactly a century later, at the beginning of Alexander's supremacy, Ant. xi, 7, 2. Whichever date be correct, this was most probably the occasion from which the Samaritan Pentateuch had its origin. Perhaps the most important divergence which it makes from the Hebrew text—the reading of Gerizim for Ebal in Dt. 27, 4— was made at the same time. The present value of the Samaritan Pentateuch lies in this, that at whatever time it was obtained from the Jews, that is at the latest probably about the year 433, these latter still employed the old script. Yet there is nothing historically impossible in the old view which looked upon the Samaritan Pentateuch simply as the Law which had existed in both Judah and Israel from much earlier times. In that case it would contribute nothing to the subject of discussion.

3. *In the Other Books.* However the case may have been with the Law, the other books continued to be written in the old script after Ezra's time. The reference to the jots and tittles of the Law, Matt. 5, 18, rather gains point, if we suppose them to have been confined to it. The book of Esther (8, 9) speaks of the Jewish language and writing as peculiar to them. The Jewish language can only mean the language of the book of Esther—Hebrew, and the Jewish writing, as distinguished from the Aramaic at the time in use throughout the Persian Empire alongside of the cuneiform, can only be the old Hebrew character. In the book of Daniel, which is generally now dated 165 B.C, there is the writing on the wall which could not be read except by a Jew. The Chaldeans used Aramaic: the other writing must be intended to be old Hebrew.

4. *Evidence of LXX.* The LXX translation is hardly evidence for the script of Palestine seeing that it was made in Alexandria. The Law was probably translated as the tradition states in the reign of Ptolemy II, and by the middle of the second century B. C. the complete translation of the Old Testament into Greek had been accomplished, at least so far as it existed and was known to Ben Sira[1]. Variations of the LXX from the Hebrew, due to mistaking one letter for another, point to an early form of the square character as that in which the copies used by the LXX were written. But, as has been said, the Jews of Egypt employed the Aramaic script in the second century B.C. if not before, and this does not prove that the same script was in use in Palestine equally early.

5. *Evidence of Text Itself.* A better source of evidence is found in the variations between parallel passages in the Hebrew text itself. The best examples of these for the present purpose are found in the lists of proper names, as for instance of the cities of the Levites in Josh. 21 and 1 Chr. 6, or of David's heroes in 2 S. 23 and 1 Chr. 11, or in the genealogical trees in the books of Chronicles and those in the other books. Gesenius in his 'Geschichte der hebräischen Sprache und Schrift' § 43 gives the following amongst others:

1. Confusion of ב and כ, Neh. 12, 3 and 14, Shechaniah and Shebhaniah: 11, 17=1 Chr. 9, 15.

ו and י, Gen. 36, 27=1 Chr. 1, 42.

כ and ם, 1 K. 7, 41=2 Chr. 4, 11, 16.

---

[1] Ecclus. prologue.

CHAPTER III.

ב and ר, Ps. 18, 12 = 2 S. 22, 12.

ז and ן, Ps. 31, 3 = 71, 3.

נ and ר, Ezra 2, 2 = Neh. 7, 7: Nebuchadnezzar and Nebuchadrezzar.

נ and ס, 2 S. 23, 35 = 1 Chr. 11, 37.

ן and ת, Num. 26, 35 = 1 Chr. 7, 20: Josh. 21, 32 = 1 Chr. 6, 61.

2. ד and ר, Ps. 18, 11 = 2 S. 22, 11: Lev. 11, 14 = Dt. 14, 13 and very often.

3. ב and ד, 2 S. 23, 29 = 1 Chr. 11, 30.

The consonants most frequently confused in the Hebrew text are ד and ר which are very much alike both in the old and in the new scripts. ב and ד on the other hand are more similar in the old, but they also resemble one another in the earlier though not in the later Aramaic. The other examples point to the square character for their origin, and may be taken as proving that, when these errors arose, the books were written in that character. But the question is, When did these errors arise? They arose subsequently to the date of the LXX translation, for they are not found in that translation with rare exceptions. Of all the instances which Gesenius cites only one clear case of the Greek reproducing the error of the Hebrew text occurs and that one is from the books of Samuel (II, 22, 11). These books became corrupt at a very

JEWISH AND OTHER COINS.

SHEKEL OF SIMON MACCABÆUS. Silver.

HALF-SHEKEL. Silver.

 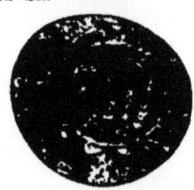

COIN OF AUGUSTUS, struck at Antioch, and known in the New Testament as the Assarion or Farthing. Bronze.

DENARIUS OF TIBERIUS—The "Penny." Silver

SMALL JEWISH COIN OF ALEXANDER JANNÆUS, probably the "Mite." Bronze. 105—78 B.C.

early date and to a greater extent than any other book in the Old Testament.

Hence the divergent readings of parallel passages of the Hebrew text instead of proving the square character to have been in early use, show that the books in which these divergences occur were not written in that character until after the completion of the LXX translation, that is until about the middle of the second century B. C. at the earliest.

6. *Conclusion.* After the testimony of the Talmud, the main argument for the ascription of the introduction of the square character to Ezra, is the belief that after his time the script was regarded as sacred and could not have been changed. It is very doubtful whether this was the case. The coins of the periods of the Maccabees and of the last Jewish war would certainly have been struck in the sacred script if a sacred script had existed at the time, but their legends are in the Hebrew language and in the old Hebrew script, although those of Herod were stamped in the Greek language and character; so it is not a case merely of the retention of a practice obsolete elsewhere, like the retention by the Arabs of the Cufic character on their coins or in the titles of the Surahs of the Koran long after the present script was in use for other purposes, or like the retention of Latin on some of our coins. It points rather to two scripts having been in use at the time, like the Roman and black-letter types in Germany, or like the Arabic and Roman systems of numerals. The old Hebrew letters seem to have been used for business purposes long after the square character was used exclusively for sacred purposes. Moreover, the old script was more legible to western foreigners than the new. And the Talmud permits Jews resident outside of Palestine to possess copies of the Law in Coptic, Median, Hebrew, Elamitic and Greek. Here 'Hebrew' can only mean the old Hebrew script, not the language, and the other terms must mean scripts also.

CHAPTER IV.

THE PRESERVATION OF THE TEXT.

1. *Internal Conditions.* The Jews were well, indeed, named by the Arabs one of the peoples of the Book. Ever since the discovery of the book of the law in the temple at Jerusalem in the reign of Josiah in the year 625, or it may have been centuries before that date, their religion has been inseparably bound up with a book; but from the time of the return from Babylon the religion of Palestine became an attempt to fulfil to the letter the written word. And when the national centre of that religion was destroyed, the whole soul of the nation was thrown into, and for centuries absorbed in, the study of the Book. Hence it comes about that, whereas no manuscript of any part of the Jewish Scriptures older than the tenth century is known to exist in the original language, yet by means of citations from them in Jewish works of the second century and earlier, by means of quotations in the New Testament and, still more, from the LXX translation it is possible to show that the consonantal text as it existed at the beginning of the Christian era was substantially what it is now. Although the Jews of that and later periods do not seem to have had any scruples about transliterating it into other scripts or even translating it into other languages, such as the Muslims have in the case of the Koran, yet they evinced a regard for the letters of the original text themselves almost amounting to superstition. It seems to have been the transliterated copies of the Jewish Scriptures for use in countries outside Palestine that suggested to Origen the idea of the second column of the Hexapla, which represents the Hebrew text in Greek letters[1]. Origen lived from 185 to 254. All the most important Greek translations of the Old

---

[1] Blau, Heilige Schrift p. 81.

Testament were made by Jews—the LXX, those of Aquila, Theodotion and Symmachus—and had for their object a nearer approximation in sense to the Hebrew —that of Aquila being so extremely literal that it can hardly be called Greek. For example, in Gen. 1, 1 he translates את הארץ by σὺν τὴν γῆν. The Syriac (Peshitto) version is also apparently the work of Jewish or of Jewish-Christian hands.

2. *External Circumstances.* In addition to the great labour expended in the attempt to arrive at the exact sense of Scripture, external circumstances also conspired to preserve the purity of the text. As persecution purifies the Church, so it at the same time purifies its literature. Even a persecution directed against the books themselves, like that of Antiochus Epiphanes, while reducing the number of copies only increases the care bestowed in emending and protecting those which survive.

There are three moments in Jewish history at which the existence of their sacred literature was especially endangered. The first was that which ended in the destruction of Jerusalem and the Temple under Nebuchadnezzar in the year 587 B.C. Amongst the plunder carried away to Babylon, books are not named, but they must surely have formed part of it, for the captives themselves would cling to them. We know the names of some books which no longer exist and which may well have perished at this time. Such is the Book of Jashar mentioned Josh. 10, 13 Hebr. 2 S. 1, 18 and 1 K. 8, 53 LXX. Both this and the Book of the Wars of Jehovah (Num. 21, 14) were probably collections of lyrics, chiefly war-songs, such as the Lament of David over Jonathan, which would naturally, amongst the Jews as amongst other peoples, form the beginnings of literature. It is often supposed that it was during the Exile that the early historical materials were worked up into something of their present shape as found in the books from Genesis to Kings, after which the sources of this compilation may have been discarded as separate books. Similarly the Law is supposed to have been reduced to its present form in the years following the return from the Exile.

The second epoch at which the Jewish sacred literature was brought into jeopardy of its existence was that of the persecution under Antiochus Epiphanes. This was the first religious persecution to which the Jews were subjected from without, and the only one for centuries. Antiochus ordered all copies of the Law or even of any of the books to be destroyed; and any person found in possession of a copy of the former was liable to capital punishment, 1 Macc. 1, 56. 57, Jos. Ant.

xii. 5. The author of Chronicles appears to mention a considerable historical and biographical literature which has not survived.

For a third time the Jewish Scriptures were seriously imperilled on the occasion of the capture of Jerusalem by Titus and the destruction of the Temple. But by this time the Law at least had long been a definite fixed quantity, which had been minutely studied and commented upon, to such an extent that if every copy had perished it could have been restored from memory. Besides, ever since the exile there had existed a Jewish colony in Babylon, where the scriptures were as eagerly studied as in Palestine, if not more so. According to the Babylonian Talmud the copies of the Law were destroyed by Titus, but Josephus (Wars vii, 5, 7) states that one copy had a place in the triumph of Vespasian. In this copy, which is the earliest manuscript of the Law known as having existed, there are said to have been thirty-two trivial variations from the received text, some of which are said to have been found also in a manuscript belonging to R. Meir of the second century. Some idea of the slightness of the variations which attracted notice even at this early period may be obtained from the following examples:

Gn. 18, 21: for 'its cry' read 'their cry'.

24, 7: for 'my native land' read 'my land'.

48, 7: omit the reference to Bethlehem, Rachel's tomb being in Benjamin.

Dt. 29, 22: omit 'Admah and Zeboim'.

Vespasian's manuscript was deposited in the royal palace at Rome and subsequently in the year 220 handed over to the synagogue of Asverus, i. e. Severus, most probably the emperor Alexander Severus who was a good friend to the Jews.

The other scriptures were not considered so sacred as the Law, but they were considered sacred and minutely studied. Jerome mentions a various reading in Is. 21, 11 of Rumah, i. e. Rome, for Dumah: in a manuscript belonging to R. Meir it was also found. It is stated that at one time only three manuscripts of the Law were left and that a text was obtained by the simple method of choosing in every instance of diversity the reading of two against one. Josephus (Life 75) states that he obtained from Titus a gift of the sacred books after the fall of the City.

Doubts have been cast upon these statements of Josephus and others, and such early accounts are generally simply discarded. But that such a process of ascertaining and fixing the true text, especially of the Law, was thus early gone through is clear from the result—that there are no various readings in the Hebrew text of the Old Testament in the sense in which we speak of various readings in the New. Attention is drawn to this fact in the preface to the Revised English Version.

3. *The LXX Version.* There is only one of the ancient Versions which has any claim to come into competition with the Hebrew original as a witness to the text, and that is the LXX. This claim rests upon two grounds. In the first place the Greek manuscripts are centuries older than the Hebrew—the former of the fourth, the latter of the tenth century. Secondly, the LXX was made long before a uniform Hebrew text such as we now have existed—from the middle of the third to the middle of the second century B. C., whereas there is no evidence for the existence of a uniform Hebrew text before the first century of our era. At that time the Hebrew and Greek Bibles lived together in Palestine, and the Apostles quoted either indifferently, so little did their divergences affect the sense. Apart from the Apocrypha it is only in the Book of Jeremiah and in the later chapters of Exodus that the Greek differs very widely from the Hebrew. In the former the Greek is the shorter by one eighth of the whole, but this is mostly effected by dropping certain constantly recurring formulae; though the order of the chapters is also completely changed, and it is a question whether the Greek is a condensation of the Hebrew, or the Hebrew an expansion in Rabbinic style of the original text. In the case of the other books the LXX forms an invaluable aid towards the restoration of the text in those places where it has become corrupt, especially in those books where the translator does not seem to have been able to make any intelligible sense of the original.

CHAPTER V.

DESCRIPTION OF TEXT OF FIRST CENTURY.

1. *Purely Consonantal.* In order to obtain some idea of the appearance which the Hebrew text presented at the period of its first reduction to uniformity about the beginning of the Christian era, it is necessary to remember that the script at this time consisted solely of consonants, in an early form of the square character, resembling that of the earliest inscriptions in that character. The letters may have been much smaller than we are used to, for Jerome complains of their being trying to the eyes. The different books were written on separate rolls. By 'books' in the Old Testament we must understand rolls or *volumes*, as in Is. 34, 4 'the heavens shall be rolled together as a scroll', ספר. The word מגלה is not used before the time of

Jeremiah and then only in a few passages. Jesus was handed the roll of the prophecies of Isaiah, Luke 4, 17. Most of these volumes were the property of the synagogues: private persons rarely possessed one, but acquired their knowledge of their contents in the schools and from hearing them read in the synagogues, where the Law was read through regularly once in three years and accompanied by extracts from the prophets. The text ran on continuously without division into chapters or, probably, verses; but the words were separated by an interstice as well as indicated by the use of final letters. The four vowel letters were used more sparingly in the earlier, regularly in the later books, but there were no other vowel-signs. The text consisted wholly of the twenty-two consonants, except that a few words were marked by the scribes with one or more dots placed over them.

2. *Word-Separation.* On the Moabite Stone and Siloam Inscription the words are divided by means of a point. This point is found also in the Samaritan Pentateuch; so that it was still employed by the Jews in the year 433 or possibly later, that is, at whatever date the Samaritan Pentateuch was obtained from them.

On coins both Samaritan and Jewish, on gems and Phœnician inscriptions generally, it is not found, nor

DESCRIPTION OF TEXT OF FIRST CENTURY. 43

on Aramean Inscriptions. In these last, with the exception of the Palmyrene, the words are divided by a space. It is natural to suppose that when the Old Testament autographs were written in the old Hebrew character they had this point, but that when they began to be written in the square character the use of the point was dropped. Hence it frequently happens that letters are combined to form one word instead of two, and the converse. There are fifteen places mentioned by tradition, where two words are written as one. They are Gen. 30, 11 בגד for בא גד: Ex. 4, 2: Dt. 33, 2 (text corrupt): Is. 3, 15 מלכם for מה לכם: Jer. 6, 29 should read מאש תם 'is consumed of fire': 18, 3: Ezek. 8, 6: Ps. 10, 10 חלכאים 'weak persons,' for חל כאים, 'a host of afflicted': Ps. 55, 16 (15) the text means 'let desolations be upon them': 123, 4: Neh. 2, 13: 1 Chr. 9, 4: 27, 12: Job 38, 1 and 40, 6, where מן is written in full, as would always be done at first like the Arabic article, even although the ן is assimilated to the following consonant, cf. the Latin inl.=ill. Other examples are Jer. 44, 18 מן או: Joel 1, 12: 1 Chr. 5, 18 מן בני and frequently. One word is written as two in Jud. 16, 25: 1 S. 9, 1: 24, 9: Is. 9, 6: 44, 24: 2 Chr. 34, 6: Lam. 1, 6: 4, 3.

Other passages in which tradition and the text differ, are 2 S. 5, 2 היתה מוציא for המוציא הית: Ezek. 42, 9: Job 38, 12: Ezra 4, 12.

The LXX, based as it was on an Aramean text in which the dividing point was not used, frequently groups the letters differently from the Hebrew. Examples are:

Hos. 11, 2 Hebrew מפניהם From before them.
   Greek מפני הם From before me. They...
1 Chr. 17, 10 Hebrew ואגד לך And I told thee,
   Greek ואגדלך And I shall make thee great.
Ps. 106, 7 Hebrew על ים By the sea,
   Greek עלים Going up.
Ps. 73, 4 Hebrew למותם At their death,
   Conjecture למו תם To them. Perfect[1]...

3. *Other Breaks in the Text.* Neither was there any indication to mark the end of a verse, other than the same space which was used for the end of a word. For frequently the verse division is wrong or the LXX divides differently from the Hebrew, just as in the case of words. Thus in

Gn. 49, 19, 20, instead of, 'overcome at the last. Out of Asher ....' we must read, 'press upon their heel. As for Asher ...,' making the first letter of v. 20 the last of v. 19.

Ps. 42, 6, 7: 'His countenance. O my God,' should be, 'my countenance and my God,' as in v. 12 and 43, 5. And so some texts read.

---

[1] For other examples cf. Driver p. XXXI.

DESCRIPTION OF TEXT OF FIRST CENTURY. 45

Jer. 9, 5, 6: instead of, 'Thine habitation is in the midst of deceit', שבתך בתוך מרמה, The LXX join the first two letters to the previous verse, '(weary themselves) to repent. Oppression upon oppression, deceit (upon deceit),' נלאו שב: תך בתוך מרמה במרמה.

Ps. 90, 2, 3: 'Thou art God. Thou turnest (man to destruction).' The LXX read 'Thou art. Turn not...' which accounts for the jussive תשב and so, too, in verses 11, 12.

If the word or verses had been divided by a point the variations with the LXX and the evident wrong divisions should have been fewer: if there had been no indication at all, they should have been more frequent. The conclusion is that words and verses were divided simply by a space.

Moreover, there was in the text of the first century no division into chapters or even books. The Psalms themselves were not separated at first, so that their number is now doubtful. The Authorized English Version follows the Hebrew. But the Greek makes one Psalm of 9 and 10 and of 114 and 115, at the same time splitting 116 and 147 each into two. The Syriac follows the LXX with regard to 114 and 147, thus still preserving the total of 150. Some manuscripts join together Psalms 42 and 43. Ps. 1 does not seem to have been counted, for in Acts 13, 33 the Codex Bezae calls the second Psalm the first.

4. *The Final Forms of Letters.* Connected with the indication of the division of words is the use of special final forms of letters. In the old Hebrew of the Siloam Inscription there are no special final forms. These are a necessary result arising from the employment of ligatures between the letters which modify the forms of the letters which they unite. Ligatures begin to make their appearance in the Egyptian Aramaic and the Palmyrene. Hence in some of the Egyptian Papyri of the second century B.C. there is found a distinction between the initial and medial and final forms of *kaph*, *lamed* and *nun*. Final *nun* is also found in the earliest square Hebrew inscriptions, that is, in the first century. Final *mem* and *pe* are not found in any inscription until the end of the third century. But it is known from other sources that by the first century five special final forms had been accepted and the rest rejected. These were, in alphabetical order, ך ם ן ף ץ. In all except ם the final form is obtained by turning down again the tails, which were in the Phœnician originally vertical, but which had in the later Aramean scripts begun to curve towards the left, so that in form the final letters are a return to the more archaic type. In the case of ם the same process may not have been adopted for fear of confusion with final ף. There seems to have been a disinclination to end a word with a stroke drawn to meet the next word. The final letters obviate this.

5. *Origin of Final Letters.* Before the end of the second century only one of the Jewish sages attempts to account for the genesis of the final consonants, Mathiah ben Ḥarash (a pupil of R. Eleazar who died in the year 117 A.D.). He said that Moses received them on Mount Sinai; so, by the middle of the second century the final letters were regarded as of authority. In the third century they were credited to the prophets. The letters themselves are often referred to in the Talmud and by Jerome. The Samaritan Chronicle of the eleventh century says that Ezra not only changed the script but also added five new letters, that is, he invented the final forms.

But the final consonants are not so old as the LXX translation—at least as parts of it. Frequently where that translation divides the words or verses differently from the Hebrew it is a question as to the place of one of the letters with final forms, whereas if such forms had been in use there could have been no doubt as to which word the letters belonged to. A good example is Jer. 23, 33. The Hebrew has את מה משא, 'what burden?' which makes no sense. The Greek reads correctly אתם המשא, 'Ye are the burden.' Other examples are the following, the Hebrew text reading being given first;—

   1 S. 1, 1 בן־צוף Son of Zuph: LXX In Nazif בנציף.

   1 S. 20, 40 לך הביא Go, bring: LXX Come now, come לכה בוא.

   Ps. 44, 5 אלהים צוה O God, command: LXX My God is commanding אלהי מצוה.

   Nah. 1, 12 אם שלמים If at peace: LXX Ruling waters משל מים.

   Hos. 6, 5 משפטיך אור Thy judgments are light: LXX My judgments are like the light משפטי כאור.

   Ps. 16, 3 בארץ (המה) In the land: LXX In His land בארצה.

   Zech. 11, 11 וידעו כן עניי הצאן So the poor of the flock shall know: LXX And the Canaanites shall know the flock וידעו כנענים הצאן.

The reference of the introduction of the final letters to Moses or to Ezra followed naturally from the reference of the square character to the one or the other of them. The reference to the prophets has also been accounted for as follows. The Jewish schoolmasters were in the habit of forming mnemonic words composed of special sets of letters which they wished their pupils to remember, and they combined the final letters into the two words מן צפך, that is, מצופיך 'from Thy prophets.' The prophets are called watchers in Is. 52, 8: Hab. 2, 1 and elsewhere. This mnemonic word was in the third century interpreted as indicating the origin of the final letters; and it accounts for the order in which they are mentioned, which is not the alphabetic order. But the sages of the second century were also called צופים by those of the third.

6. *Talmudic Reference to Final Letters.* The statement in Ex. 32, 15, that the tables of the law were written on both sides, was interpreted to mean that the letters were cut through the stone from one side to the other. On this R. Ḥasda, † 309, said if the letters were the Assyrian or square character final ם could only have stood by a miracle, having nothing to support it. The same remark had been made before by R. Levy of the third century concerning the letter ס as well as the old Hebrew ע which was a complete circle or triangle—if the tables were written in the latter script.

7. *Conclusion.* Thus it appears that after the adoption of the square character there were no divisions in the text of the books other than spaces left between the words, and that before the first century A.D. there were frequent various readings in manuscripts in respect of word-division, but that from that date onwards the word-division of the received text was retained even where it was acknowledged to be wrong, being always written and copied, even if not read.

As to the motive which led to the use of final forms, it has been suggested that they were invented to supply ciphers for the higher numerals, ך for 500 and so on; or that they were intended to indicate the end of the words, in which case there would have been more than five. The fact seems plain that they arose naturally and spontaneously out of the use of ligatures and were retained after the ligatures were discarded. At first the final forms would occur sometimes medially and the medial forms sometimes finally, the final form being properly at the end of the ligature, not at the end of the word. Examples of this are Is. 9, 6 למרבה with a final ם: Neh. 2, 13 המ with a medial מ: מנ is so written in Job 38, 1: 40, 6: לבנ 1 Chr. 27, 12 (cf. above p. 43). There would no doubt have been three forms of letters, initial, medial and final as in Arabic and Syriac, if the Hebrew script had not crystallized so early.

8. *The Vowel-Letters.* The consonant used to represent a vowel sound came to be called אם למקרא or אם הקריאה, that is, *mater lectionis*. The four consonants so employed are אהוי and they seem to have been used from the time when writing first began. On the Moabite Stone the תי of the 1st pers. sing. pf. of the verb and the ו of the 3rd pl. and the י of the constr.

pl. are all written with the *scriptio plena*, and ו and י are also used freely in the middle of a word. In the Siloam Inscription all four vowel-letters are used, but the writing is still more defective than that of the manuscripts. It is possible that inscriptions were spelled more defectively in order to save expense, whilst in writing on leather the vowel-letters may have been fully used from the first as in Arabic. Hence perhaps it is that the Samaritan text is even more fully equipped in this respect than the Jewish.

In the text, however, as it existed in Egypt in the end of the third and beginning of the second century B.C., the vowel-letters were not so plentiful as in the present text, for the copies used by the Greek translators omit them in many places where they now stand. Thus in Amos 9, 12 they translate אדום by τῶν ἀνθρώπων, and in Ezek. 32, 29 they read for the same word ארם, Syria: in Hos. 12, 12 for שורים, oxen, they read שרים, princes; which they could not have done if the ו had been written; and so frequently.

On the Jewish coins of the second century B.C. and the second century A.D. all four vowel-letters are found, thus, ירושלים, יהודים, קדשה, ראש.

In the received text itself some slight advance may be detected on comparing the older and later portions in this respect. Thus דויד, שלוש, רכוש are mostly written defectively in the earlier books, fully in the later. דויד is always so written in Chronicles, Ezra and Nehemiah. Cf. also קרתן in Josh. 21, 32, more defective than on the Moabite Stone, which has קרתין: elsewhere it is קריתים in the received text, 1 Chr. 6, 61 (76).

9. *Anomalous Forms.* By the first or second century the vowel-letters were considered inviolable and so left standing in the text wherever they were found, even when regarded as wrong: see Hos. 4, 6: Mi. 3, 2: Hos. 8, 12: and 9, 16 and often, except in the Torah, in which Dt. 32, 13 seems the only instance. But generally the vowel letter represents another possible pronunciation of the word.

The Pentateuch is peculiar also in that in it the 3rd pers. sing. fem. pronoun היא occurs only eleven times, הוא being written instead in the other 195 places, cf. Gen. 2, 12 and 14, 2. Outside the Law הוא is masculine, though the tradition makes it feminine in Is. 30, 33 unnecessarily: in 1 K. 17, 15 and Job 31, 11 הוא and היא exchange their vowel sounds.

This phenomenon has never been satisfactorily explained. Originally both הוא and היא were written simply הא as on the Moabite stone. It is suggested that הוא may have been of common gender, which is unlikely, since all the Semitic languages have the two forms. It is more probable that היא=הוא is a survival from that phase of the square character in which the letters ו and י are identical, and that the apparent ו is really an old י, and conversely. In Ps. 73, 16 and Eccl. 5, 8 היא seems to stand for הוא, though it may be otherwise explained in both passages. The rarity of היא in the Law would be explicable from its earlier reduction to a received text. היא=הוא is said to be found also in Babylonian codices of the prophets and elsewhere.

The received text has remained more defectively written than even the Moabite Stone in exceptional cases, as when the 1st pers. sing. pf. of the verb is written without the י, as in Ps. 140, 13: 1 K. 8, 48; and 2 K. 18, 20 according to Is. 36, 5: so the ה of the fem. especially in the word נערה.

Thus in respect of vowel-letters as of word-division the text was stereotyped exactly as it was found or fashioned in the first century, even when it did not conform to the rules of the prevailing orthography of the time.

10. *The Dotted Words.* When a scribe in writing or copying a book had miswritten or miscopied one or more letters or words, instead of drawing his pen through the error, and so spoiling the appearance of his manuscript, he generally placed a dot or dots over it to indicate that it was to be omitted in reading.

The copyists of the Hebrew manuscripts at the commencement of the Christian era seem to have followed a similar practice, for we find a number of dotted words in the received text of the Old Testament. These points are, however, susceptible of another explanation, according to which they arose in the course of the collation of manuscripts, and indicate words or letters which were found in some copies and not in others, and so were looked upon with suspicion and marked as doubtful; or they may even mean that the letters so marked are to be retained. If so, they represent the first attempts at Biblical criticism.

There are, in all, fifteen passages so marked in the Old Testament, ten in the Law, one in the Psalms and four in the prophets. In printed texts and manuscripts the word נקוד is placed in the margin against which one of these occurs. נקד means in later Hebrew to place points on a word, and נקוד, if pronounced *niqqûdh*, would mean 'punctuation': otherwise it is the passive participle, 'punctuated'. Or it might be the adjective *nāqôdh* used in Gen. 30, 32 of sheep and goats in the sense of 'speckled.'

11. *Their Antiquity.* As to the antiquity of these *puncta extraordinaria,* those which occur in the prophets are not known to us except from the text itself and the marginal notes found on manuscripts. The others are all mentioned in the Talmud or Midrashim, only one, however, that in Num. 9, 10, being found in the Mishnah, that is, before the end of the second century. But the explanation of the point there given only seems to show, that it was by that time a thing of such antiquity that its meaning had been hopelessly lost. The dotted words are found on the synagogue rolls, being with one exception the only signs admitted there in addition to the consonants and vowel-letters. Hence, they are older than R. Aqiba, † 135, even before whose time every book of the text was considered sacred and the addition of dots would not have been permitted. The second century commentary called Sifre can offer only traditional explanations of them. The lower limit, therefore, for their origin is the end of the first century A. D. They cannot have been later than that, and are in all probability considerably earlier. The Midrash Rabba commenting on Num. 3, 39 refers them to Ezra. It says: 'What mean the points? Ezra thought if the prophet Elijah should come and ask, Wherefore didst thou write this? I shall answer him, I have placed dots over it. If he say, Thou hast written correctly, I shall remove the points.' The points, however, are not so old as Ezra's time. An upper limit is found in the LXX translation which knows nothing of them, and in which the emendations apparently indicated as desirable are not needed.

On the whole, the most probable date for the origin of these dots seems to be the first century A. D. or the latter part of the first century B. C.

The oldest authority to refer to any of the points is Sifre[1] in a note on Num. 9, 10, according to which they indicate that the letter or letters so marked are to be deleted or transposed. But Blau thinks that the restriction of the force of the dots to a single letter is due to the tendency of feeling in the second century, by which time it was held that 'the world might be destroyed by the insertion or omission of a letter in the Torah' (Talmud Tractate Erubim 13 a &c.), and that their reference originally extended to words or even verses.

The fact that no dotted words occur in the Hagiographa outside the one in the Psalms, and only four in the Prophets, points to the greater care with which the text of the Law was collated and revised.

12. *List of Passages.* 1. Gen. 16, 5. 'The Lord judge between me and thee.' בינֶיךָ with two *yods* and a dot over the second. The correct orthography is בינך and the dot would naturally draw attention to the peculiar

---

[1] Ed. Friedmann p. 18 a.

form. But in the oldest authorities the dot is not necessarily on the י, and in a codex of the thirteenth century there is said to have been a dot on every letter, and this applies to all the other passages as well as the present. This might mean that for 'thee' we should read 'her' or 'them'.

2. 18, 9. 'And (the angels) said to him (Abraham)' ויאמרו אליו. This may indicate that אליו should be omitted altogether. The person addressed is not expressed in this chapter, which belongs to J, except in verse 13 where there is a change of subject. Or perhaps it means, 'read ויאמר לו,' singular as v. 10. But according to another tradition the dots should be on the following איה so that the passage would run, And they said to him, 'Sarah thy wife,'—and he said, 'Behold, in the tent' (interrupting). But the absence of a dot over the ל in our printed texts is probably due to there being other dots there, so that the presence of only *three* dots would be very late indeed and count for nothing. Cf. no. 11. The manuscript mentioned under 1 has a dot on the ל also.

3. 19, 33. 'He perceived not when she lay down nor when she arose.' ובקומה might mean that the word should be written as in v. 35, ובקמה. But besides the codex of 1294 mentioned above, both Rashi, 1040—1105, and

Levi ben Gerson, generally known as Ralbag, who died in 1307, testify to there being a point on every letter. Sifre does not mention there being a single point only, nor whether it is the word in v. 33 or that in v. 35 which is dotted. What it says is, בשכבה לא ידע אבל בקומה ידע, that is, ובקומה is to be omitted in both verses. Both may have been dotted originally and the note נקוד על ובקומה ב, 'dots on the two ובקומה' read as, 'dots on the second ובקומה.'

4. 33, 4. 'And Esau ran to meet him and embraced him and fell on his neck and kissed him; and they wept.' וישקהו has a dot on every letter. Some present texts omit the one from the ש on account of the diacritical point which they have. The old Jewish explanation is that they are a sort of notes of admiration and draw the reader's attention to the depth of Esau's guile; and there is a conjectural emendation וישכהו, 'and bit him.' The word is doubtful. נשק in generally construed with the dative, though not always. The LXX has, 'And Esau ran to meet him and, embracing, kissed him and fell on his neck and both wept,' transposing וישקהו and ויפל על צוארו. Many manuscripts omit the former word altogether. Cf. ch. 45, 14, 15. We may suppose the order of the LXX to be original, and that of the Hebrew to be due to its being the commoner mode of expression. Cf. Luke 15, 20. Or we may

suppose that both readings form a doublet, and that one of the terms should be struck out.

5. 37, 12. 'And his brethren went to feed their father's flock in Shechem'—אֵת צֹאן. In v. 2 רעה is followed by ב instead of את as here, but that verse is supposed to be the meeting-point of two different sources, which may spoil the construction; though רעה is construed with ב (1 S. 16, 11). The old traditional explanation of the dots given in Sifre is that the brothers went to feed themselves. This seems to mean that we should translate 'to feed on their father's flock,' or it directs attention to the other meaning of את, 'to feed along with the flock.' The explanation is wanting in the usual traditional respect for the patriarchs. Or the point may be that the flock was their own and not their father's.

6. Num. 3, 39. 'The Levites which Moses and Aaron numbered at the commandment of the Lord.' ואהרן has a dot on every letter. The intention evidently is that the 'and Aaron' is due to the constant coupling of the two names—the scribe having written 'Moses' added 'and Aaron' mechanically—and that it ought to be omitted as in vv. 14, 16 and 40. It is wanting in the Samaritan Version and some of the old translations but it is found in the LXX. That Aaron did take part with Moses in the census appears from chap. 1, 1—3.

7. 9, 10. 'If any man of you or of your posterity shall be unclean by reason of a dead body, or be on a journey afar off, yet shall he keep the passover unto the Lord.' Here 'a journey afar off' is דרך רחקה and there is a dot on the ה. This is the only one of the fifteen dotted words explained or mentioned in the Mishnah (Tractate Pesachim, 92 b) where in answer to the question, What is a far journey? one Rabbi says, 'From the threshold of the Temple court and outward,' and another adds that this is the meaning of the point over the ה—that it does not really mean 'far' but has the technical force of 'outside the sacred precincts.'

Perhaps the point is meant to draw attention to the absence of any epithet qualifying journey in v. 13. Perhaps it is intended to indicate that the masculine רחק is to be read instead of the feminine רחקה, דרך being of common gender. Blau thinks the dot was originally on the או, which itself was originally ו, and was intended to signify that either of these two disqualifications was sufficient, by itself, to prevent one from eating the passover; and it was not necessary that both should occur together. Possibly the text originally ran בדרך רחק הלך לכם instead of בדרך רחקה לכם cf. v. 13. The dropping out of letters when identical letters follow would explain it.

8. 21, 30. 'We have laid them waste even unto Nophah

which reacheth unto Medeba': 'which reacheth'=אשר
with a dot on the ר, clearly suggesting the deletion of
the ר and the reading of אש: 'with fire unto Medeba.'
The LXX has πῦρ but read the remaining words quite
differently. The Samaritan also read אש. The text
is probably corrupt.

9. 29, 15. 'And a several tenth deal to each lamb.'
The first עשרון has a dot over the ו, and elsewhere the
ו is omitted (28, 13). Blau thinks the note, 'delete
ועשרון,' was read, 'delete ו עשרון,' that is, 'delete the ו
of עשרון,' and that the whole word should be omitted.

10. Dt. 29, 28 (29). 'The secret things belong unto
the Lord our God but those things which are revealed
belong unto us and to our children for ever,' לנו ולבנינו
עד עולם with eleven dots extending from לנו to the ע
of עד. Sifre explains: 'The points mean if ye fulfil the
revealed laws I will reveal unto you the hidden also.'
So Blau points and omits ליהוה אלהינו, that is, 'The
hidden things and the revealed belong unto us...' The
number of dots is the same as the number of letters
in ליהוה אלהינו: they would be removed from a dislike
to having them placed over the divine names.

11. Ps. 27, 13. '(I had fainted) unless I had believed
to see the goodness of the Lord in the land of the
living.' There is nothing corresponding to 'I had fainted'
in the Hebrew, and the word 'unless,' לולא, is dotted

with three points above and four below. As the text stands it presents an incomplete sentence, being a protasis without an apodosis, which, however, is not unparalleled. The LXX (26, 13) had only the לו of לולא, which they attached to the preceding verse. Only the Targum supports the present reading. The marginal note (which is very late) נקוד מלמעלה ומלמטה חוץ מן וו שלא נקוד אלא מלמטה is translated by Baer: 'Pointed above and below except vav which is not pointed except below.' This note presupposes the vowel points already existent, otherwise there would be no motive for not pointing the *vav* above, except the fear of confusion with *ḥolem*. Blau translates מלמעלה ומלמטה 'at the beginning and at the end,' i. e. of the whole verse, and thinks they were confined to the first word from a dislike to interfere with an entire verse. He omits חוץ וגו' as being later. Or, perhaps, the last word חיים fell immediately below לולא and the dots placed over it became attached to לולא below, for this is the only instance of a word being dotted below. The dots thus signify that the whole verse is in its wrong place and must be transferred.

This verse is mentioned in the Talmud (Berachoth 4a)—'David said before the Holy One, blessed be He, Lord of the world, I am confident in Thee, that Thou wilt pay a good reward to the righteous in the world to come, but I do not know whether I shall have a part with them.' This points to the reading לי לא.

12. 2 S. 19, 20. 'My lord the king went out of Jerusalem.' יצא has a dot on each letter. There is no explanation. Perhaps it stands for גלה or יצאת.

13. Is. 44, 9. 'And they are their witnesses: they see not.' ועדיהם המה בל יראו but המה has a dot on each letter. It is probably an error of dittography and should be omitted as in the Syriac, so that the passage runs, 'And their witnesses do not see.' The LXX omits the whole clause.

14. Ezek. 41, 20. The word ההיכל, the Temple, is written twice, ending v. 20 and commencing v. 21, and the former is dotted, So, for 'the wall of the Temple,' read simply 'the wall.' Several manuscripts and the LXX, Syriac and Vulgate versions omit the word.

15. 46, 22. 'These four corners were of one measure.' The Hebrew word translated 'corners' really means 'cornered,' cf. A.V. margin. But it has a dot on every letter except the ו and is to be omitted, as it is by the LXX. Read, 'one measure to the four of them,' or read as at the beginning of the verse.

13. *The Inverted* נ*'s*. In two passages verses are marked with the letter נ inverted. In Num. ch. 10 an inverted נ stands at the beginning of v. 35 and another at the end of v. 36. In Ps. 107 an inverted נ stands at the beginning of vv. 23—28 and 40 in the best texts. In the marginal note at the foot of the page (which is very late) such a נ is called נ הפוכה, turned upside down, or נ מנוזרה, turned back to the front.[1] The Talmud (Shabbath 115 b) speaks merely of סימניות i. e. σημεῖα. Soferim uses the word שיפור, *shippûr*, of unknown meaning. Sifre on Num. 10, 35, 36 speaks of the verses as being marked with dots at the beginning and end. The *nuns*, therefore, here and in Ps. 107 were originally dots and stand for נקוד, and have in these two passages the same force as the dots in Ps. 27, 13, that is, they are equivalent to brackets and indicate that these verses are not standing in their proper place. So Sifre, שלא היה זה מקומה. The explanation of Rabbi, that these two verses form a book by themselves, comes to the same thing. In the LXX vv. 35 and 36 precede v. 34.

14. *Large and Small Letters.* Another feature of the consonantal text of the first century is the occurrence of large and small letters. Some of these are referred to in the Talmud. Large letters seem to have served various purposes, sometimes corresponding to our capitals, as at the commencement of books. In

---

[1] Delitzsch explains, singled out, i. e. peculiar.

Lev. 11, 42 the ו which is written large is the middle letter of the Law, as the note in modern editions says. In Deut. 6, 4 the Israelite's Credo is similarly marked, but probably late, the motive being liturgical. According to the Talmud, Gehenna is prepared for him who pronounces this verse indistinctly. In Dt. 32, 4 הצור, the Rock, has a large צ; but in v. 6 the large ה in הל יהוה seems to indicate the reading הליהוה: the other places are Gn. 1, 1: 30, 42: Ex. 34, 7, 14: Lev. 11, 30: 13, 33: Num. 13, 30: 14, 17: 27, 5: Dt. 18, 13: 29, 27: Is. 56, 10: Mal. 3, 22: Ps. 80, 16: 84, 4: Pr. 1, 1: Job 9, 34: Cant. 1, 1: Ru. 3, 3: Eccl. 7, 1: 12, 13: Esth. 1, 6: 9, 6, 29: Dan. 6, 20: 1 Chr. 1, 1.

Instances of minuscules are Gen. 2, 4 בהבראם with a small ה pointing apparently to the various reading בבראם: 23, 2 &c.

Buxtorf's *Tiberias* gives thirty-one large, and thirty-two small letters. The traditional explanations are fanciful. Thus, the small ה in Gn. 2, 4 is to indicate that all created things are small and perishing; or it is remarked that by a transposition of letters it is possible to read באברהם, 'for the sake of Abraham,' i. e. of the chosen People; and so the small כ in 23, 2 is to indicate that Abraham did not weep to excess for Sarah. The other cases are 27, 46: Ex. 23, 19: 32, 25: 34, 26: Lev. 1, 1: 6, 2: Nu. 25, 11: 31, 24: Dt. 31, 27: 32, 18:

Is. 44, 14: Jer. 14, 2: 39, 13: Nah. 1, 3: Ps. 27, 5: Pr. 16, 28: 28, 17: 30, 15: Job 7, 5: 16, 14: 33, 9: Esth. 9, 7, 9: Lam. 1, 12: 2, 9: 3, 36: 4, 14: Dan. 6, 20; but all editions do not reproduce all these.

15. *Suspended Letters and Divided Nun.* A suspended letter is called אות תלויה. There are four.

Jud. 18, 30: 'Jonathan the son of Gershom the son of Manasseh,' is read in all the versions except the Vulgate, but in the Hebrew text the נ of Manasseh is written above the line, reminding readers that the name should be Moses and the נ an early insertion intended to save Moses from being the grandfather of an idolater, and to reflect upon the idolatrous king Manasseh.

Job 38, 13 and 15, רשעים is twice written with the ע suspended, but probably only the ע of the second רשעים was meant. ב='second' being mistaken for ב='two'. The earliest explanation—that of Simon ben Lachish of the middle of the third century is that ראשים, 'chiefs', should be read, which fits in better with the parallel member: ראשים for רשים 'poor', would also make sense.

Ps. 80, 14 (13): 'The boar out of the wood doth waste it.' The ע of יער is suspended. One explanation is that it points to a various reading יאר, the Nile, i. e. Egypt. More probably it denotes the middle letter of the Psalter like the large ו in Lev. 11, 42. This can only be proved by counting the letters. The passage was later referred to Christianity and connected with the eating of swine's flesh and the Crucifixion.

In Num. 25, 12 the ו of שלום is cut in two, אות קטיעה, 'I will give unto him (Phinehas) my covenant of peace,' to indicate that the covenant was broken when the high-priesthood, between Eli and Abiathar, passed to the line of Ithamar, after which it returned to that of Phinehas.

16. *Abbreviations.* Abbreviations are found on early Jewish inscriptions and also on coins on which ש=שנה, the numerals being denoted by the letters of the alphabet, so that שב means, 'in the second year': יש stands for ישראל, and so on. It has been suggested [1] that in the Hebrew text used by the LXX the letters ה ם ת, when final, were not written; for the LXX frequently have the 2nd sing. perf. where the Hebrew has the 2nd pl. in תם or they read a singular for a plural or the converse, e. g. in Prov. 2, 20 for בדרך טובים, 'in the way of good men,' they have τρίβους ἀγαθάς = בדרכם טובים: 16, 13 מלך for מלכים: 13, 19 תאות for תאוה and so on.

There is evidence that the proper name יהוה was written in the text used by the LXX simply י. In Ps. 31, 7 (6), LXX 30, 7, 'I hate them that regard lying vanities, and as for me I trust in Jehovah,' we must

---

[1] Lagarde, Anmerkungen zur griech. Uebersetz. Proverb.

read with LXX, Peshitto and Vulgate, 'Thou hatest,' as Ps. 5, 5, and the י stands for יהוה, with which אני is contrasted. In Jud. 19, 18 for the Hebrew בית יהוה the LXX have 'My house,' and in Jer. 6, 11 and 25, 37 for 'the anger of the Lord,' they have 'My anger,' treating the י as the suffixal pronoun instead of a contraction of יהוה.

The variations, however, which are most easily explicable on the supposition of the employment of abbreviations in the Hebrew text, seem to occur with greatest frequency in the book of Jeremiah, in which the LXX is shorter by one eighth than the Hebrew, so that it is possible to explain them on that ground. Moreover, the fact that the LXX regarded letters as forming abbreviations does not prove that they were so meant. In Jer. 3, 19 for the Hebrew איך, How! they have γένοιτο κύριε ὅτι, i. e. אמן יהוה כי, but the other is correct and their interpretation wrong.

That abbreviations were at least rare, is shown by the fact that variations arising from the supposed apocopation of plural and feminine terminations are exceptional, and also by the fact that proper names involving such terminations are correctly transliterated by the LXX[1]. In any case the employment of ab-

---

[1] They have 'Ιεροβοάμ=ירבשה 2 S. 11, 21.

breviations belongs to the period before the unification of the text in the first or second century.

Although there are no numerical ciphers on the Moabite Stone or the Siloam Inscription, it is likely that numbers were indicated either by letters of the alphabet, as on Jewish coins, or by ciphers, as on Phœnician coins and Palmyrene inscriptions. The supposition is necessary to explain the great corruption existing in those parts of the text concerned with numbers. Only explicable thus are:—1 K. 4, 26 (Hebr. 5, 6) 40,000 stalls for horses = 2 Chr. 9, 25, 4,000.

2 S. 10, 18 700 chariots = 1 Chr. 19, 18, 7,000.

2 S. 24, 13 seven years of famine = LXX and 1 Chr. 21, 12 three.

2 Chr. 21, 20 and 22, 2: Jehoram dies aged 40 leaving a son aged 42: read 22 as 2 K. 8, 26, that is, כב for מב.

Compare also Ezra II and Neh. VII. Perhaps in this way the excessively high numbers in the Pentateuch are to be accounted for, as well as the variations between the Hebrew, Greek and Samaritan, for example in Gen. 5.

17. *Summary.* Such in all probability was the Hebrew text of the Old Testament as it existed at the beginning of the Christian era. It was a Received Text obtained by the collation of manuscripts and by the rejection of various readings. From that time onwards all copies are identical, reproducing even the marked errors of the original. Yet before that epoch no such uniformity existed. The Greek version often differs widely, and the Samaritan considerably, from the present text. The Book of Jubilees—of the middle of the first century—shows variations from it "not inferior in extent to those still existing in New Testament manuscripts," and even in the second century various readings still survived. But the standard text, backed by the scribes, quickly superseded all rival copies, so that not one remains. So too the Koran existed at first in different recensions in different countries, until, in the thirtieth year of the Muhammedan era, the Khalif Othman caused a number of copies to be transcribed from the copy which had belonged to Abu Bekr, and to be circulated through the provinces, all other copies being destroyed.

As to how far the scribes were fit to form a text, they appear to have possessed the all-important qualification of fidelity to the letter. The corrections which they felt themselves bound on grounds of reverence to apply to the text were extremely slight. Otherwise we may be pretty sure that they allowed nothing to be written for which there was not manuscript authority: and the principle on which they went seems to have been the simple one referred to above, of adopting the reading of the majority of manuscripts.

No clearer proof could be had of the literal fidelity of the scribes to their manuscripts than the fact that the text at which they arrived contained numerous errors, contradictions and inconsistencies. With their microscopic acquaintance with the text, they cannot have failed to observe how frequently parallel passages fly in the face of one another, and yet they allowed all these defects to stand. Some of these are due obviously to intentional alterations of the text and some are merely due to such scribal errors as arise in the course of transcription.

CHAPTER VI.

ALTERATION OF ORIGINAL DOCUMENTS.

A. INTENTIONAL ALTERATION.

1. יהוה *and* בעל. The most striking variation between parallel passages, and the one which is of most frequent occurrence, is that of the Divine name in the Psalter. The proper name of the God of Israel was composed of the four consonants יהוה. In the first Book of Psalms, I—XLI, this tetragrammaton occurs 272 times: אלהים is scarcely used as a proper name, whereas in the following Psalms XLII—LXXXIII, יהוה occurs only 44 times: אלהים 200; as if these Psalms belonged to a later period than the first, when the name יהוה was considered too sacred to be used and אלהים was substituted for it. Compare especially Ps. 14 with Ps. 53 and Ps. 40, 14—18 with Ps. 70: Ps. 50, 7 with Ex. 20, 2. The change is even made where it makes no sense and it is necessary to restore יהוה to understand the passage, e. g. 50, 7. In the fourth and fifth Books of Psalms, XC to CL, יהוה is again used and אלהים may be said not to occur. This could be explained by supposing these Psalms to be still later than the second group and to belong to a period when the pronunciation of the tetragrammaton had been lost, so that whilst יהוה was regularly written, אלהים or אדני was read instead of it, as is done amongst the Jews at the present day. Where אלהים does occur in the two last Books it occurs in citations or compilations, Pss. 108 and 144, and is allowed to stand simply because there was no reason for not allowing it to stand. On the other hand in Pss. 53 and 70 there was, on the above hypothesis, a reason for changing יהוה into אלהים. Compare outside the Psalter 2 K. 22, 19 with 2 Chr. 34, 27. The result is that to this day the correct pronunciation of the Divine name is unknown. The change of יהוה into אלהים is original, that is, it was made by those who composed or compiled the Psalms in question and it is found in the LXX. But it is not implied that all the Elohim Psalms once existed as Jehovah Psalms.

Another alteration precisely parallel to the foregoing was made in the case of proper names compounded with that of the adversary of Jehovah—Baal. 'Baal' is properly a common noun meaning lord, master or husband, and it was in early times regularly used by worshippers in addressing Jehovah. But on the rise of the Phœnician Baal worship in Israel, the application of the name Baal to Jehovah was forbidden by the prophets. Thus in Hos. 2, 16 (18) it is said, Thou shalt call Me אישי and shalt no more call Me בעלי. Both אישי and בעלי mean 'my husband', but the latter was not to be applied to the God of Israel. The prophets often refused to use the word even of the Phœnician deity and preferred to write בשת, Shame, in place of it, Jer. 3, 24: Hos. 9, 10, and even when Baal formed one of the components of a proper name it might be changed into Bosheth. The name of Saul's surviving son was Ishbaal, i. e. man of Baal, i. e. of Jehovah; but in 2 S. 2—4 he is called Ishbosheth. Later still, when the idolatrous connotation of the word בעל had been forgotten and no objection was seen to Israelitish names being compounded with it, we get back to the original form once more, Eshbaal (1 Chr. 8, 33: 9, 39). The same process is seen in the case of Mephibosheth (2 S. 4, 4 and 1 Chr. 8, 34) Elyada (2 S. 5, 16 and 1 Chr. 14, 7 cf. 3, 8) and Jerubbaal (Jud. 6, 32, 8, 35: 2 S. 11, 21). Here, too, as apparently in the case of the name יהוה, there are the same three phases of use, disuse and resumption of use. In the oldest period (Jud. 8, 35) בעל is admitted into Israelitish names: in the second (2 Sam.) it is excluded and בשת substituted for it; and in the third (Chronicles) בעל is re-admitted.

Here also the LXX follows the Hebrew text and their habit of placing the feminine article before בעל, ἡ βαάλ, is to be explained by the equivalence of that expression to ἡ αἰσχύνη. The vowels of the name Molech are the same as those of בשת and are probably derived from it. Perhaps it was originally Melech=King, and latterly pronounced Bosheth.

2. *Euphemistic Expressions.* Here and there are found several expressions of a euphemistic character which can scarcely be original; e.g. in 1 K. 21, 10 (LXX 20, 10) 'Thou didst blaspheme God and the king,' for 'blaspheme' both the Hebrew and the Greek have 'bless'. The word translated 'curse' in Job 1, 5: 2, 5 and 9 is the word elsewhere translated 'bless' in the Hebrew, and some equivalent euphemistic expression in the Greek. In some passages on the other hand קלל, to curse, is used (Ex. 22, 27: Jud. 9, 27: Is. 8, 21 [1]). With the former practice may be compared the name Euxine for the Black Sea and the Arabic البعيد منك, he who is far from you, i. e. the person addressed.

Or the objection to coupling 'curse' with 'God' or 'King' was met by inserting the expression 'the enemies of' between them, 2 S. 12, 14 where the A. V. 'given great occasion to the enemies of the Lord to blaspheme' is an impossible paraphrase: it can only mean, 'Thou hast greatly despised [the enemies of] the Lord.'

Another use for the latter device is found e. g. 1 S. 25, 22, where an imprecation is invoked on the enemies of David. The expression 'the enemies of' is not found in the Greek and has been inserted because David's threat was not fulfilled.

In 2 S. 24, 1 David is instigated to number the people by the Lord, in 1 Chr. 21, 1 by Satan: 1 Chr. 17, 13 passes over the chastising of Solomon of 2 S. 7, 14: 1 Chr. 17, 11 alters the coarse expression in 2 S. 7, 12. Perhaps in the well known passage Gn. 49, 10 'until Shiloh come' or 'until he come to Shiloh,' the text may have been altered.

3. *The Tiqqûn Soferim or 'Correction of the Scribes'*. תקון is an abstract word meaning 'correction' and not

---

[1] In none of these does the word 'God' immediately follow the word 'curse'.

'a correction' in the concrete. And the תקון סופרים means the correction which the scribes before the Christian era applied to the consonantal text, after which date the text was regarded as inviolable and unalterable. In Jewish works on the text, mention is made of from eleven to eighteen places in which the text was altered by the early scribes, without any indication being left to show that it had been altered. These are called י"ח דברים (מלין) תקון סופרים, 'the eighteen words by correction of the scribes.' The changes were dictated by a sense of propriety and reverence and a desire to avoid anthropomorphic expressions, and were in all cases effected by the alteration of a single letter or at most of a word.

1. Gn. 18, 22 'But Abraham stood yet before the Lord,' is said originally to have run, 'But the Lord stood yet before Abraham.' To stand before one is an oriental posture of deference.

2. Nu. 11, 15 'And let me not see my wretchedness,' was originally, 'Thy wretchedness,' that is, the wretchedness caused by Thee. Sifre, the Jewish commentary of the second century, still had the reading 'Thy wretchedness.'

3. Num. 12, 12. The text apparently ran, 'And let us not be as one dead, (us) of whom the flesh was half-consumed when it came out of our mother's womb,'

instead of the present. 'And let her not be as one dead, of whom the flesh is half consumed, when he cometh out of his mother's womb.' That is, read .... נהי תהי ... בשרו ..... אמו instead of בשרנו ...... אמנו. The Syriac (of second century) read, 'And let us not be.' The motive for the change would be to exclude the high priest.

4. 1 S. 3, 13 'because his sons made themselves vile', A. V. is an impossible translation of the Hebrew מקללים להם, itself an impossible construction. For להם read אלהם=אלהים, 'did revile God'. This is the reading of the LXX. Jewish tradition gives the alternative 'did revile Me' which comes to the same thing, and does not mean that לי should be read for להם, for קלל is not construed with the dative, but is merely the Jewish way of indicating that אלהים should be read.

5. 2 S. 16, 12 'It may be that the Lord will look upon mine affliction.' The Hebrew consonants בעוני can only mean 'upon my iniquity' or 'upon my punishment;' but they were read בעיני, 'upon my eye,' of which the Jewish interpretation is 'upon my tears,' as in the A. V. margin and the Targum. The LXX, Syriac and Vulgate all agree with the A. V. text, but this requires us to read בעניי. According to the tradition, however, the correct reading is בעינו 'with His eye,' which was

felt to be too anthropomorphic and the י and ו were transposed. Cf. no. 10.

6. 2 S. 20, 1 'Every man to his tents, O Israel.' It is said that 'to his tents' should be 'to his God.' The change is effected by merely transposing two letters, לאלהיו for לאהליו. Similar expressions occur 1 K. 12, 16 and 2 Chr. 10, 16. The motive for the change would be a disinclination to admit the existence of polytheism in ancient Israel. But 'to his tents' seems clearly to be the true reading, though we should expect the singular, 'to his tent.'

7. Ezek. 8, 17 'Their nose' for 'My nose'[1], to avoid anthropomorphism as also in

8. Hab. 1, 12 'Art Thou not from everlasting, O Lord my God, mine Holy One? We shall not die,' for 'Thou wilt not die.'

9. Mal. 1, 13 'Ye have snuffed at it,' for 'at Me.'

10. Zech. 2, 12 (A. V. 8) 'He that toucheth you touches the apple of his eye,' for 'My eye.' In Dt. 32, 10 'He kept him as the apple of His eye,' the reference of the pronoun is ambiguous: so it is allowed to stand. Cf. no. 5.

11. Jer. 2, 11 'My people have changed their glory for that which doth not profit,' for 'My glory;' but 'their Glory' might mean Jehovah, and יועיל reflect on בעל.

---

[1] Cf. חמם probably for חמי Jer. 51, 39.

12. Job 7, 20 'I am a burden to myself,' for 'I am become a burden upon Thee,' as the LXX reads. For עלי cf. Pss. 142, 4: 143, 4 &c. for עליך cf. Am. 2, 13.

13. Hos. 4, 7 (the same as no. 11) 'Therefore will I change their glory into shame.' 'My glory' would require the further alteration, 'they have changed.' But 'their Glory' may be Jehovah: and 'Shame,' קלון, might mean Baal. But most likely the text is to be interpreted without any special references.

14. Job 32, 3 'And yet had condemned Job,' for 'condemned God,' איוב for אלוה. There is a dislike to connecting the Divine name with the verb to condemn &c. cf. under section **2**.

15. Lam. 3, 20 (as no. 12) 'My soul ... is humbled in me,' for 'is humbled for Thee' or 'meditates upon Thee.'

16. Ps. 106, 20 (the same as nos. 11 and 13).

It will be observed that there are only sixteen passages though the number eighteen is mentioned. The discrepancy is to be accounted for either by the occurrence of more than one point for correction in no. 3 or by reckoning the parallel passages to no. 6. Ten are 'corrected' by altering the suffixal pronoun. In four cases there is an interchange of ו and י, which letters in the oldest form of the square character are identical. As, with two exceptions, nos. 4 and 12, the LXX ignores the supposed original form of the text the alterations must have been made, if at all, at an extremely early period, in the fourth or beginning of the third century B.C. Yet in two instances, nos. 2 and 3, a tradition of the unemended form lingered on until the second century.

4. *The 'Iṭṭûr Soferim.* In the same category with the תקון סופרים falls the עטור סופרים. This word means 'subtraction' and denotes the removal by the scribes of a letter which they considered an insertion of the unskilful. There are only five passages, from each of which the scribes removed the conjunction 'and', in Gen. 18, 5: 24, 55: Num. 31, 2 and Ps. 68, 25 (26) from before the word אחר, and in Ps. 36, 6 (7) from before משפטיך 'thy judgments,' the text having read originally 'and afterwards' &c.

B. UNINTENTIONAL ALTERATION OF ORIGINAL DOCUMENTS: CLASSIFICATION OF SCRIBAL ERRORS.

The consonantal text of the Hebrew Bible as it existed in the first century and as it exists still, is not to be compared with a modern version. The latter is obtained by the collation of a great number of manuscripts and of older versions, the defects of one manuscript or of one version being corrected by the others, until errors are almost entirely eliminated, so that the text obtained though identical with no one source, is brought as near perfection as is possible. According to a late tradition mentioned before, at one time only three copies of the Law were available, and a text was obtained from these, not by selecting what seemed to be the best reading in each case, based on a consideration of the authority of the different manuscripts, but simply by adopting the reading of two against one. Hence it comes about that the Hebrew consonantal text resembles not so much a version as a Manuscript. It is practically a Hebrew Manuscript of the first century; and like the most of human achievements it exhibits many imperfections, displaying all the ordinary errors and defects found in manuscripts. These have been classified in the following manner:—

1. *Failure to understand the Sense.* a. WRONG DIVISION of words. Besides the passages mentioned above where the Greek text or the Tradition departs from the Hebrew text, there are a number of passages where the words are almost certainly wrongly divided, and where the error cannot have escaped observation, although the versions do not supply the correction, e. g. Am. 6, 12, 'Shall horses run upon the rock? will one plow there with oxen?' so A. V. supplying 'there': 'with oxen'=בבקרים which might also mean 'in the morning hours' (so August Müller) but more likely it is two words run

into one: translate, 'Do men plough the sea with oxen?', בבקר ים.

Jer. 15, 10 כלה מקללוני is unparalleled: read כלהם קללוני.

Jer. 22, 14 חלוני ו׳, 'windows and...' read 'his windows', חלוניו.

Ps. 73, 4 (given above p. 44).[1]

b. MARGINAL NOTES finding their way into the text. Of this source of error there is no indisputable example in the Old Testament text, but attempts have been made to emend difficult passages by resort to it. In Ps. 40, 8, 9 'Then said I, behold I come (in a volume of a book it is written of me) to do Thy will &c.' it has been suggested[2] that the parenthetical clause is a marginal note referring to the word לי in v. 7 and mentioning that in one roll it is written עלי.

In 2 S. 1, 18 it is said of the lament of David over Saul and Jonathan, 'he bade them teach the children of Israel the bow'. Verse 6 states that Saul was attacked by chariots and horsemen (literally, 'masters of horses,' בעלי הפרשים, where בעלי is superfluous). In 1 S. 31, 3 Saul is said to have been attacked by archers. Wellhausen suggests that verses 6 and 18 stood opposite to one another in adjacent columns and a scribe noting the omission of any mention of archers in v. 6

---

[1] For other examples cf. Driver p. XXX.
[2] By T. K. Abbott.

wrote, on the margin בעלי קשת of which בעלי found its way into v. 6 and קשת got into v. 18.

2. *Errors due to the Eye.* a. REPETITIONS. 2 Sam. 6, 3, 4 the last word of v. 3 and the first five words of v. 4 have been accidentally repeated from v. 3. Omit with LXX.

Lev. 20, 10 omit the five words repeated: so Ex. 30, 6 (LXX).

1 Chr. 9, 35—44 is repeated from 8, 29—38.

Is. 41, 1 'renew their strength' is from last verse of ch. 40.

Is. 53, 7 omit the second, 'so he opened not his mouth'.

See also 2 S. 17, 28: 1 K. 6, 8: 2 S. 23, 8 cf. 1 Chr. 11, 11: 2 S. 21, 19 cf. 1 Chr. 20, 5. In Josh. 21 verses 36, 37 (A. V.) are omitted from the text but found in the margin, cf. 1 Chr. 6, 78, 79: according to the tradition also eight words are inserted which should be omitted.

b. OMISSIONS. 1. Supplied by parallel passages: 1 Chr. 8, 29—31 supplemented by 9, 35—37: see 9, 41 A. V.

Josh. 22, 34 'called the altar Ed', name supplied from 24, 27 by the Syriac.

2. Supplied by Versions. Pr. 10, 10b comes from v. 8: read with LXX and Syriac, 'He that rebuketh boldly is a peacemaker:' In Pr. 11, 16 between a and b the LXX and Syriac insert. 'But a woman that hateth

F 2

righteousness is a seat of disgrace. Slothful men do lack substance,' and read 'diligent' for the Hebrew 'violent' in the next half verse, חרוצים for עריצים.

2 S. 17, 3, for the Hebrew 'The man whom thou seekest is as if all returned,' the Greek has, 'As a bride returneth to her husband: thou shalt seek only the soul of one man.'

Job 23, 12 'I have esteemed the words of his mouth more than my necessary food,' מחקי: מחקי צפנתי אמרי פיו should go with the first half of the verse, and add בחיקי=בחקי in the second, 'Neither have I caused the command of his lips to depart from my right, I have hidden the words of his mouth in my bosom.' Job 27, 18 'He buildeth his house as a moth,' should be 'as a spider,' i. e. עש should be עכביש.

3. Tradition notes the omission of ה 45 times and of vowel letters often, also of ten entire words.

c. TRANSPOSITIONS 1. Of letters: Josh. 6, 13 הולך for הלוך. The tradition mentions sixty-two such cases of transposition of ו: 2 K. 14, 6: Jer. 9, 7: Ps. 73, 2 &c.

Is. 8, 12, קשר 'conspiracy' should be 'holiness' קדש cf. vv. 13, 14.

1 S. 14, 50, 51: A י has slipped from one line into the one above it so that Abner is called Abiner and בן is read for בני. This is very curious, and it is found in the LXX. It is one of many indications that there

was a uniform text in Egypt long before there was one in Palestine.

2 Chr. 3, 4 makes the porch of the Temple 120 cubits high! For מאה ועשרים read אמה עשרים, 20 cubits, with the LXX. Cf. 1 K. 6, 2.

2. Of words: Ps. 35, 7 reads, 'They have spread a pit, their net they have digged.' Transpose שחת and רשתם.

3. Of verses: Is. 38, 21 and 22 should come next to v. 8: cf, 2 K. 20, 6—8.

Most cases of omission and insertion are due to homœoteleuton or homœoarchton.

d. Similar letters mistaken for one another. The most common are ד and ר, ו and י, ב and ד, ה and ח.

Ps. 110, 3 wavers between בהדרי קדש and בהררי קדש, 'in holy attire' and 'on holy mountains.' Tradition[1] mentions four places where ר is written instead of ד, 2 S. 13, 37: 2 K. 16, 6: Jer. 31, 40: Pr. 19, 19: two places where ד is written for ר; and two where ח is written for ה: ו and י are interchanged in 154, ב and כ in 11 words.

Other examples are Josh. 9, 4 ויצטירו, 'made as though they had been ambassadors,' ויצטידו 'took provisions':

---

[1] They are given in Okhlah ve Okhlah, no. 123.

Dt. 14, 13 הראה 'the glede,' for Lev. 11, 14 הדאה 'the vulture': 2 Chr. 22, 10 ותדבר for ותאבד (2 K. 11, 1).

3. *Errors due to the Ear.* 2 Chr. 10, 18 Hadoram for Adoram 1 K. 12, 18: also the constant interchange of על and אל. Tradition mentions fifteen places where לא should be לו, *viz.,* Ex. 21, 8 : Lev. 11, 21 : 25, 30 : 1 S. 2, 3: 2 S. 16, 18: 2 K. 8, 10: Is. 9, 2: 63, 9: Ps. 100, 3: 139, 16: Job 13, 15: 41, 4: Pr. 19, 7: 26, 2: Ezr. 4, 2. Cf. also Is. 49, 5: 1 Chr. 11, 20: 1 Sam. 2, 16: 20, 2. Thus in Ps. 100, 3 'and not we ourselves' should be 'and His we are'. יהוה and אדני would also sound alike in reading.

4. *Failure of Memory.* This would explain the use of different but synonymous words in parallel passages without any apparent motive, as אקרא in 2 S. 22, 7 and אשוע in Ps. 18, 7, and the interchange of יהוה and אדני in certain cases. In Jer. 27, 1 Jehoiakim should be Zedekiah, cf. v. 3 and ch. 28, 1.

5. *Errors due to Carelessness or Ignorance.* Gen. 36, 2 'Anah the daughter of Zibeon': *daughter* should be *son*: so Sam. LXX Syr. and v. 24.

Nu. 26, 8 'And the sons of Pallu; Eliab' is simply carelessness: the scribe wrote on as in the preceding verses without looking ahead. So in 1 Chr. 3, 22 and often.

1 Chr. 6, 13 (28) 'And the sons of Samuel; the first-born Vashni and Abiah.' *Vashni* means 'and the second': the first-born was Joel, 1 S. 8, 2.

1 S. 13, 1 'Saul was   years old.' The number has dropped out. From the text it was most likely fifty נ ['one year old' is generally בן שנתו].

Is. 21, 16 perhaps the same thing has happened here.

2 S. 3, 7 'Ishbosheth' has fallen out of the text: the LXX Syr. and Vulg. have it.

2 S. 23, 18, 19 the first 'three' should be 'thirty' (as in Syriac).

2 Chr. 22, 6 כי has to be translated as a preposition.

Ezek. 43, 13 has also to be corrected by the LXX.

The text of the Books of Samuel exhibits more errors due to this cause than any other part of the Old Testament. This is probably due to their being not so much used for public edification, but very much read privately on account of the intrinsic interest of the narrative.

6. *Conclusion.* The received Jewish text of the Old Testament in the first century had the merits and defects of an unpointed manuscript of that period. No attempt was made then or subsequently to clear it of even manifest corruptions and inconsistencies. Even combinations of letters which did not form words were retained and read somehow. The small changes which are said to have been made by the scribes do not seem to have been regarded as approaching nearer to the original form, but rather as a concession to the spirit of the times. From the second century onwards, the consonantal text was regarded as sacred—the world might stand or fall by the omission or insertion of a letter in the Torah. The result is that the consonantal text of the second century is precisely the consonantal text of the present day. The forms of the character became modernized and great changes in the way of the introduction of additional signs were made, but no letter was added and no letter was taken away.

CHAPTER VII.

PROGRESS OF HISTORY OF TEXT DURING FIRST SEVEN CHRISTIAN CENTURIES.

1. *All Study of the Text was Oral.* The consonantal part of the Hebrew Text of the Old Testament was practically fixed in the first or at latest in the second Christian century, and it has remained substantially unchanged ever since. During the first six centuries the text was studied and minutely commented upon; all such study being carried on orally. The Mishnah which was completed in the year 190 by R. Jehuda the Holy was not then written down but was preserved solely by memory and tradition. By the end of the fifth century the other part of the Talmud, the Gemara, or commentary on the Mishnah, was completed. But even this huge compilation was preserved orally and the reduction of it to writing long forbidden. The History of the Hebrew Text during this period is almost a blank. The text itself as written remained at the end of the fifth century substantially unchanged in appearance from what it was in the first—a bare consonantal text. This was considered holy and unalterable; and to preserve it the numbers of the words, 79856, and even of the letters, variously put at from 350,000 to 600,000, occurring in the Law, were counted sometime during the early centuries, so that nothing might be lost or added, and the other books were similarly dealt with.

 2. *The text not always Read as Written.* The scribes did not always read the words of the Scriptures exactly as they found them on the written page. From one motive or another they changed a word in the reading and read something else. This practice began at a very early date—in fact very soon after the return from Babylon, and had its root in subjective motives. At last it grew up into the system of marginal readings found in modern printed texts and known as *qrê* or *qrî*, of which the plural is *qaryan*. *qrê* is pass. pc., *qrî*, impt. of the Aramaic *qrâ* meaning to read. It has to be noted that we have not yet reached

the period when these readings were reduced to writing. When that occurred, they had existed for centuries and were passed on from generation to generation by tradition. It is with these *qrîs* in their oral and unwritten state that we have now to do. In so far as they may have been based on various readings found in ancient manuscripts, they have a real manuscript value only inferior to that of the text. But in so far as they have no such foundation, they rather resemble the errata and corrigenda in modern printed books, but without the authority of these: in fact, they stand in the same category with the conjectural emendations of a present day critic.

The earliest case of a word being read differently from what it was written is that of the name יהוה. The motive for this proceeding may be found in Lev. 24, 11 where the punishment for the irreverent use of the Divine name is death. Here the expression used is ויקב את השם, which may mean either 'blasphemed the name' (as the A. V., from קבב) or, better, 'pronounced the name', as Jewish tradition explains it, from נקב in the sense of to *define accurately, name,* cf. Gn. 30, 28. This expression השם is the original of the post-Biblical ה׳ for יהוה. Even before the commencement of the LXX translation, that is, before the middle of the third century B. C. יהוה was no longer pronounced; for that translation has κύριος for it, i. e. אדני. Apparently for this very reason there was no longer any hesitation about writing the name since it was not uttered. The discontinuance of its use may have been due to the growth of religion as much as to a sense of reverence. As soon as the God of Israel was recognised, as He is recognised by the earliest prophets whose writings have come down to us, as being not one among many national deities, but the only God in heaven and earth—any proper name became unnecessary. Hence, from a very early period wherever this proper name occurred it was read by the Jews אדני or, where that word immediately preceded or followed, אלהים. The κύριος of the New Testament is derived from this usage through the LXX.

Very frequently the written text was departed from in reading, in order to substitute a more refined expression for a coarser. Instances are Dt. 28, 30: 2 K. 18, 27: 1 S. 6, 11. But in the great majority of cases the reading departed from the written text on grounds of grammar or logic. Thus:—

a. A word was frequently read which was not written: Jud. 20, 13: 2 S. 8, 3: 16, 23: 18, 20: 2 K. 19, 31, 37: Jer. 31, 38: 50, 29: Ruth 3, 5, 17 (see chap. VI no. 2).

b. Or, a word was omitted in reading: 2 S. 13, 33: 15, 21: 2 K. 5, 18: Jer. 38, 16: 39, 12: 51, 3: Ezek. 48, 16: Ru. 3, 12.

c. The letters of a word were transposed as ו in sixty-two passages, Josh. 6, 13 (see above p. 84).

d. One letter was substituted for another; this is especially the case with ו and י. The cardinal instance of this is הוא for היא in the Pentateuch.

e. Words were divided differently in the reading and in the writing. Examples have been given above under the Division of Words, p. 43.

3. *Means to Preserve the Text.* Besides fixing how the text was to be read the scribes of this period also took measures for the preservation of the text. For this purpose they counted the number of verses and even of letters in the various books and noted which was the middle verse or letter. They also began to make mental lists of words which were written in some abnormal manner. The middle verses of books will be found Josh. 13, 26: Jud. 10, 8: 1 Sam. 28, 24: 1 K. 22, 6: Is. 33, 21. In the Law the middle verse is Lev. 8, 7: the middle of the words between דרש and דרש in Lev. 10, 16: the middle letter the large ו in Lev. 11, 42. The middle verse of the Old Testament, in the traditional order of the books, is Jer. 6, 7.

The scribes also noted when a word was written abnormally—with more or fewer than the regulation number of vowel-letters, as קאם for קם Hos. 10, 14: חטאות for חטאת Jer. 5, 25: רעה for רע Mic. 3, 2: אבי

for אביא Mic. 1, 15: עני for עיני Is. 3, 8: חסידיך for חסידך Ps. 16, 10: במותי for במתי Dt. 32, 13.

All this study was oral: nothing was written down. Above all, nothing was placed on the sacred page beyond the bare text as it existed in the first century.

CHAPTER VIII.

DIVISION OF THE TEXT.

At first the only breaks in the text of the Old Testament were the spaces left between the individual words: except for these the letters ran on continuously from the first letter of a book to the last; and as each book was written on a separate leather roll and there were as yet no verses, there was no necessity for any further marks of division.

1. *Verses.* The division of the text into verses seems to have originated in the requirements of interpretation. The practice of accompanying the public reading of the Law in Hebrew with a translation into the spoken Aramaic began immediately after the return from the Exile, Neh. 8, 8. The question would at once arise, How much of the text should be read before the translator gave his paraphrase. In the Mishnah it is said: 'The reader should not read less than three verses of the

Law. Also he should not read more than one verse at a time to the interpreter. On the other hand, in the prophets he should read three verses at a time, yet only if the three verses are not three sections.' The word for a verse in the Talmud is פסוק.

But while verses existed and were recognised even in Mishnic times, they long remained without any mark to indicate where one verse ended and another began, and the placing of any such mark in the synagogue rolls has always been forbidden. The earliest indication of verse-division was a space like that which was employed to separate words. This space is called פסקא. It is found in twenty-eight passages in the middle of the present verses to indicate that some divided the verse at this point. A list of these various verse-divisions is given by Baer on Hos. 1, 2. That the verse-separation was not more clearly indicated than that of the words is proved by the frequency with which the versions and especially the LXX depart from the Hebrew text in that respect, Hos. 4, 11: Is. 1, 12 &c.

2. *Sections of the Law.* It is stated in Acts (15, 21) that 'Moses of old time hath in every city them that preach him, being read in the synagogues every Sabbath day.' The practice of reading regularly through the Law seems to have commenced immediately after the return from the Captivity, and has continued until the

present day. In Palestine the custom was to get through the whole Law once in three or three-and-a-half years: in the Babylonian synagogues once every year. For this purpose the Law early became divided into sections called *parâshahs*. These are known to the Mishnah though no distinction is there made between sections of different length. In MSS and printed texts we find the Law divided into

1) 54 long sections, although it was not until after the fourteenth century that the practice of the annual reading of the Law became universal. The divisions now fall at Gn. 6, 9; 12, 1 &c.

The Law was also divided into two other kinds of sections probably for convenience of reference merely, like our chapters, namely

2) 379 shorter paragraphs, the division being indicated by a space equal to about six or seven letters. This kind of section was called סתומה, that is, *stopped* or *closed*, because the next began on the same line.

3) 290 longer paragraphs with a space of about eighteen or nineteen letters between each, or else indicated by the next section beginning on a new line, whence they are called פתוחה, *open*.

Thirteen of the 54 sections coincide as to their

commencement with thirteen of the stopped sections, thirty-five with open sections.[1]

The Palestinian division was into 154 sections called *sedhârim,* סדרים (Job 10, 22) i. e. rubrics.

These 54 or 154 sections or annual pericopes correspond exactly to the 30 *ajzâ* of the Koran; but they sometimes destroy the sense as in Ex. 6, 28.

3. *The Haftârahs.* After the reading of the Law in the Synagogues a suitable passage from the prophets was read (Luke 4, 17). From Maccabæan times 54 passages have been selected for this purpose, called הפטרה, *dimissio.* The prophetical books were also divided into paragraphs, but the places of division are doubtful. Cases of wrong division are Hag. 1, 15: Is. 56, 9.

4. *The Poetical Books and Passages.* In all the most important manuscripts of the LXX version of the Psalms, these are written στοιχηδόν, the στίχοι being intended to correspond to the members of the Hebrew parallelism. Other books written in the same way are

---

[1] Hence they are indicated in printed texts by, ס (stopped) פ (open) סספ (stopped and one of the 54) פפפ (open and one of the 54) or where there is no coincidence, a catchword, Gn. 47, 28. But any indication except the blank space is unwarranted and unauthorized. The סדרים are indicated only at the end of the text. Baer's text has the פ and ס outside the Law, but not the old texts.

Proverbs, Ecclesiastes, Canticles, Job and the two Wisdoms. This method of writing, however, seems not to have been taken over from the Hebrew manuscripts, but to have been of indigenous growth.

In the Hebrew text of the Old Testament, certain poetical passages, and also some catalogues of names, were written in a peculiar manner, even in Talmudic times. Such are the Song of Moses in Ex. 15, of Deborah, Jud. 5, of David, 2 S. 22, and others. These songs are written 'a half-brick upon a brick and a brick upon a half brick' (Megillah 16 b), the lines consisting of two and of three parts of a verse alternately, those which consist of three parts having only one word on either side, that is, the songs are written in three columns representing the bricks in the wall of a house. Sometimes they are written in two columns as Dt. 32, or 'a half brick upon a half brick, and a brick upon a brick.' So also the lists Josh. 12 and Esth. 9.

That the Psalms as a whole were not written in this way, but continuously like the prose books, appears from the variations of the versions from the Hebrew and from one another, in respect of the division of the verses and the number of the lines (65, 8: 90, 2, 11).

5. *Number, Order and Names of the Books.* The Palestinian Jews reckoned the NUMBER of their sacred

books at twenty-four: the total given in Josephus, obtained by joining Ruth to Judges, and Lamentations to Jeremiah, was due to an effort after forced conformity with the number of letters in the Hebrew alphabet. Until about the third century A.D. each book generally formed a scroll by itself, so that the question of the order of the books had not arisen. In the Hebrew Bible the Law is counted as five books, each one named after its opening phrase. Thus Genesis is בראשית: Numbers, במדבר or, according to Jerome וידבר, which is more likely. Samuel, Kings and Chronicles form each one book. The first is called ספר שמואל, not ספרי, and its middle verse is 1 S. 28, 24. The present practice of reckoning two books of Samuel &c. arose with the Greek translation, perhaps being due to the exceeding bulkiness of the rolls containing these books in that language, for private use. The same is true also of Ezra and Nehemiah. The Hebrew book of Ezra includes Nehemiah, the latter being unknown either to the Talmud or to tradition. It is to be noted that the XII Minor Prophets constitute a single book, the middle verse being Mic. 3, 12. The Psalms would always from the time of the final redaction be written upon one roll, but the division into five books is ancient. It had already been made by the time of Chronicles; for 1 Chr. 16, 35, 36 quote Ps. 106 with the doxology which concludes the fourth book, though it has been questioned which is the original. Perhaps it was based upon the fivefold division of the Law; but if Ps. 106, 48 is a quotation, there are no longer five books.

When leather rolls gave place to parchment books of leaves sewn together and bound into volumes, the possibility of having the scriptures in a single book arose, and with it the question of the ORDER of the various writings. The change from roll to book form probably took place about the third century A. D.

In the Talmud the books are arranged and classified as follows: The whole XXIV Books are called המקרא (=Al Koran) and are divided into three parts, *viz.*;—

   I. THE LAW or תורה: five books, with a space equal to four lines between each.
  II. THE PROPHETS or נביאים: sub-divided into
     a. FORMER (ראשונים): four books; Joshua, Judges, Samuel and Kings:
     b. LATTER (אחרונים): four books; Jeremiah, Ezekiel, Isaiah and the Twelve Minor Prophets.
 III. THE HAGIOGRAPHA or כתובים: eleven books; Ruth, Psalms, Job, Proverbs, Ecclesiastes, Song, Lamentations, Daniel, Esther, Ezra (including Nehemiah) and Chronicles.

The Song, Ruth, Lam. Eccl. Esth. are called the Five Rolls.

CHAPTER VIII.

The traditional or 'Massoretic' order is slightly different. It places Is. before Jer. and in the Hagiographa the order is Chron., Pss., Job, Prov., Ruth, Cant., Eccl., Lam., Esth., Dan., Ezra-Neh. Either of these classifications is preferable to that of the Versions, ancient or modern, and is especially valuable from a chronological point of view. That the latter begins the Hagiographa with Chronicles explains how they came to find the middle verse of the Hagiographa in Ps. 130, 3.

Spanish MSS, as a rule, follow the Massoretic order of the Hagiographa. In German MSS the order generally is: Pss., Prov., Job, Song, Ruth, Lam., Eccl., Est.,[1] Dan., Ezra-Neh., Chr. The latter is that adopted in printed texts.

The NAMES are given from the contents as מלכים, שפטים; or from the author, as ישעיהו, ירמיהו; or from the nature of the composition, as תהלים, משלי; or, lastly, from some word in the opening sentences, as in the case of the five books of the Law or Lamentations, which is called איכה. The same is done in the Koran and often.

---

[1] The five rolls in the order of the occasions on which they are publicly read: Passover, Pentecost, 9th of Ab, Tabernacles and Purim.

CHAPTER IX.

THE VOCALIZATION OF THE TEXT.

1. *The Antiquity of the Points.* About the time of the Reformation it was the universal belief, both of Jews and Christians, that the vowel and other signs then and now found in Hebrew MSS. and printed texts were of equal value and of almost equal antiquity with the consonants. The Jewish tradition was that Moses received them orally and that Ezra and the men of the Great Synagogue reduced them to writing, and this was the opinion held by almost all the Jewish doctors of the Middle Ages. And with Christians the antiquity of these points was a necessary corollary from the doctrine of plenary inspiration. The theory that the vowel points were very much later than Ezra, and later even than the Talmud, was in modern times first broached by Elias Levita, 1468—1549, who inducted Christian divines into the knowledge of Hebrew. This gave rise to the famous controversy in the seventeenth century on the inspiration of the points. The elder Buxtorf, 1564—1629, had written a treatise in support of the theory that the points were coeval with the language and had always been in use. Ludovicus Capellus, b. Sedan 1579 d. 1658, took up the position that they had been invented by the Rabbis of Tiberias, 600 years after Christ, with a view to preserve a language which was fast ceasing to be spoken. The younger Buxtorf defended the position of the elder. The views of Capellus were denounced as likely to produce 'pessimas et periculosas consequentias.' The French Protestants opposed him as depriving them of many of their arguments against the Vulgate, so that he had to print his treatise in Holland. His view, however, is now universally admitted to be correct. And it is mostly agreed that both the vowel and accentual signs were adopted into the text about the same time. At what date did this take place?

2. *The Upper Limit.* We have seen that when the LXX translation was made, the Hebrew text did not possess even vowel letters to the same extent as it did when that text was unified in the first or second Christian century, and at neither of these dates did the text possess any system of vowel-signs beyond the four vowel letters. The same is true of the text at the time when the Syriac (Peshitto) Version was made from it in the second century. Jerome's Latin Version was made directly from the Hebrew and was published between the years 393 and 405: he died in 420. Jerome speaks indeed of accents (accentus) but by these he means not signs but modifications of sound merely. He says that he had no vowel sign to guide him and implies that he had no accentual signs either; and he excuses the LXX translators for rendering, e. g. Is. 24, 23 וחפרה הלבנה ובושה החמה, 'The Moon shall be confounded and the Sun ashamed,' καὶ τακήσεται ἡ πλίνθος καὶ πεσεῖται τὸ τεῖχος, by saying that they were 'verbi ambiguitate decepti,' i. e. misled by the absence of vowel-points. Another curious instance of the translators being ensnared by the same source of error is Is. 26, 14 'Dead men shall never live, nor shades arise.' For the second clause they have 'nor physicians arise.' The word is רפאים which, unvowelled, may mean either. The earlier Targums also point to an unvowelled Hebrew original. Lastly the Talmud knows nothing of specific vowel or accentual signs. Thus, it mentions five words of which the connection was doubtful (Gn. 4, 7 שאת &c.) proving the non-existence of accentual signs. So that by the end of the sixth century the Hebrew text was still an unpointed consonantal text. This yields an upper limit for the date of the insertion of the vowel and other signs; and further on this side it is impossible to get. It is necessary to begin from the other end and work backwards.

3. *The Lower Limit.* The earliest and greatest authority upon the vowel points and accents is Aaron ben Asher who belonged to the school of Tiberias and

flourished about the beginning of the tenth century. He died sometime before the year 989. He was the writer of a codex with all the present points and with notes on the same. This codex itself is lost but from the day of its writing it became the standard text of the Old Testament, which all subsequent copies and editions seek to reproduce. So far, however, from his being the author of the system, it was so ancient in his time that its origin was completely unknown to him. Ben Asher came of a distinguished family of Massoretes, or students of the Text, who had occupied themselves with that pursuit some 120 years before his time, and who would have handed down the origin of the points if it had been known to them.

Sepher Yezîrah, the earliest Kabbalistic work extant, of the eighth or ninth century, which would be expected to take account of vowel signs if they then existed, does not refer to them, proving that these signs were at any rate at that time regarded as an innovation, if, indeed, they existed.

4. *The Probable Date.* The earliest date, therefore, at which the pointed text is known to have existed is the beginning of the ninth century; and the latest date at which it is known not to have existed was about the year 600. Hence the date of the adoption of vowel and accentual signs into the text is generally taken to be some time about the end of the seventh century.

Such a date for the insertion of the vowel and other signs in the text is favoured, not merely by the history of the text itself, but also by that of the cognate languages. Even in the case of Greek MSS. the accents only begin to be found in those of the sixth century. In the case of Syriac there are two vowel systems. One of these consists of the five Greek vowels written very small and placed over or under the consonant after which they are to be read: the other consists of dots placed in varying relative positions. Traces of this latter system are found among the East Syrians of the fifth century. As Hebrew became less and less of a spoken language, the necessity would be more and more keenly felt of having some signs as guides to the correct pronunciation. It is likely that the use of such signs began to be taken advantage of in teaching in the schools, just as modern Arabic school books very often have the vowel points. The system adopted would require to be one which would no way interfere with the consonants. Such a system the Syriac already had, and the Jews seem to have taken it over from them. The Syriac accentual liturgical system was perfected about the same time. And not much later a precisely similar step had to be taken in Arabic. The received text of the Koran which was fixed by Othmân about the year 30 A. H. i. e. 650-1 A. D. depended far more upon oral tradition for its correct recital than the Hebrew Scriptures. For whereas in Hebrew only one consonantal sign represented two distinct sounds, the ש, in Arabic there were only fifteen signs to twenty-eight sounds. Diacritical points to distinguish these signs from each other were introduced by Al Ḥajjâj governor of Irak who ruled from 75—95 A. H., and a system of coloured dots for vowel signs for use in the Koran is ascribed to Abul Aswad who died in the year 69 A. H. The present Arabic system of diacritical and vowel signs is ascribed to the father of Arabic grammar Khalîl ibn Aḥmed (100-175 A.H.). In the best MSS. of the Koran the bare consonants are written in black ink and the uninspired diacritical and vowel points generally in red. As in the East Syriac system, these signs for the most part are made up of dots and lines.

5. *Various Systems*. The Jewish scribes adopted the same plan. It is not to be supposed that one system was valid everywhere at once. Probably every locality favoured a system peculiar to itself, and every schoolmaster may have invented one for the use of his own school. Of all these different systems, two have sur-

וְיַסְקוּן יָתֵיהּ בְּנֵי אַהֲרֹן לְמַדְבְּחָא עַל עֲלָתָא דְעַל אֵעַיָּא
דְעַל אִישָׁתָא קֻרְבַּן דְּמִתְקַבַּל בְּרַעֲוָא קֳ יְיָ ׃ וְאִם מִן עָנָא
קֻרְבָּנֵיהּ לְנִכְסַת קוּדְשַׁיָּא קֳ יְיָ דְּכַר אוֹ [נוּקְבָא שְׁלִים
יַ]קְרְבִינֵיהּ ׃ אִם אִמַּר [הוּא] מְקָרִיב יָת קֻרְבָּנֵיהּ וִיקָרִיב יָתֵיהּ
קֳ יְיָ ׃ וְיִסְמוֹךְ יָת יְדֵיהּ עַל רֵישׁ קֻרְבָּנֵיהּ וְיִכּוֹס יָתֵיהּ קֳדָם
מַשְׁכַּן זִמְנָא וְיִזְרְקוּן בְּנֵי אַהֲרֹן יָת דְּמֵיהּ עַל מַדְבְּחָא סְחֹ סְחֹ
וִיקָרִיב מִנִּכְסַת קוּדְשַׁיָא קֻרְבָּנָא קֳ יְיָ תַּרְבֵּיהּ אַלְיָתָא שַׁלֶּמְתָּא
לָקֳבֵל שַׁדְרְתָא יַעְדִינָהּ וְיָת תַּרְבָּא דְחָפֵי יָת גַּוָּא וְיָת כָּל
תַּרְבָּא דְעַל גַּוָּא ׃ וְיָת תַּרְתֵּין כּוּלְיָן וְיָת תַּרְבָּא דַעֲלֵיהוֹן דְּעַל
נַסְסַיָּא וְיָת חֲצָרָא דְעַל כַּבְדָּא עַל כּוּלְיָתָא יַעְדִינָהּ ׃ וְיַסְקִינֵיהּ
כַּהֲנָא לְמַדְבְּחָא לְחֵים קֻרְבָּנָא קֳ יְיָ ׃ וְאִם מִן בְּנֵי עִזָּא קֻרְבָּנֵיהּ
וִיקָרְבִנֵיהּ קֳ יְיָ ׃ וְיִסְמוֹךְ יָת יְדֵיהּ עַל רֵישֵׁיהּ וְיִכּוֹס יָתֵיהּ קֳ
מַשְׁכַּן זִמְנָא וְיִזְרְקוּן בְּנֵי אַהֲרֹן יָת דְּמֵיהּ עַל מַדְבְּחָא סְחֹ סְחֹ
וִיקָרִיב מִנֵּיהּ קֻרְבָּנֵיהּ קֻרְבָּנָא קֳ יְיָ יָת תַּרְבָּא דְחָפֵי יָת [גַּוָּא
וְיָת כָּל תַּרְבָּא דְעַל] גַּוָּא ׃ וְיָת תַּרְתֵּין כּוּלְיָן וְיָת תַּרְבָּא דַעֲלֵיהוֹן
דְּעַל נַסְסַיָּא [וְיָת חֲצָרָא דְעַל] כַּבְדָּא עַל כּוּלְיָתָא יַעְדִינָהּ ׃
וְיַסִּיקִינּוּן כַּהֲנָא לְמַדְבְּחָא לְחֵים קֻרְבָּנָא לְאִתְקַבָּלָא בְּרַעֲוָא כָּל
תַּרְבָּא קֳדָם יְיָ ׃ קְיָם עָלַם לְדָרֵיכוֹן בְּכֹל מוֹתְבָנֵיכוֹן כָּל תַּרְבָּא
וְכָל דְּמָא לָא תֵיכְלוּן

TRANSSCRIPTION

OF A PAGE FROM A FRAGMENTARY TRIGLOTT MS.
(IN POSSESSION OF DR. CHAMIZER, LEIPZIG.)

Targum Leviticus iii. 5—17, with Superlinear Punctuation.

vived, the Palestinian to which we are accustomed, and the Babylonian.

It is not certain whether the Babylonian was merely employed locally alongside of the generally used Palestinian, or whether it was not in general use before it was replaced by the latter. To commence with, both would be merely local varieties which spread. The existence of any other system beside the familiar Palestinian was not suspected until the year 1840. The MSS. of the Old Testament showing this other system are few in number, but one of them is the Codex Babylonicus of 916, the oldest of all known Hebrew MSS. of which the date is given. It was found in the Crimea by Firkowitzsch, a Karaite Jew.

Seeing that it is not certain whether this system was in general use among the Babylonian Jews, it is preferable to call it the superlinear system, since almost all its signs stand over the consonants—the reverse of the Palestinian as far as the vowel-signs go at any rate.[1] It is peculiar in having no separate sign for *e* (seghol), using *a* or *i* instead. It has, moreover, only one accentual system for all the books, in which respect it again presents a contrast to the Western system, since the latter makes a distinction like that drawn in the

---

[1] A specimen page of this system is prefixed to Baer's edition of the text of the book of Job.

Greek Church between the notation of the Psalms and of the Gospel, or between the chant and the recitative in the Latin Church.

6. *Various Recensions.* Neither was there at first one universally accepted recension any more than one universal system of vocalization. Another authority equal to Ben Asher was R. Moses ben David ben Naphtali his contemporary. Ben Naphtali belonged to Babylon, as Ben Asher to Tiberias. He also wrote a codex which, however, like Ben Asher's is lost— unless we are to believe the colophon of a St. Petersburg MS. which claims to have been written by him in the year 922. Hence arose an Eastern and Western Recension. Baer gives in his edition lists of their divergences. They are slight and mostly confined to the pointing. No doubt these two recensions, like the two systems of punctuation, are the relics of a much greater variety.

CHAPTER X.

THE PALESTINIAN SYSTEM.

1. *The Living Language.* The different systems of vowel-points and accents were attempts to stereotype the language as it had been handed down by tradition. Since it was not, however, until the end of the seventh century that this punctuation was introduced into the text, it could not but be that considerable changes had taken place, in the way of degeneration in the language, since the time when it was more of a spoken and less of a dead language.

Information as to the pronunciation of the language in earlier times may be found first of all in the transliteration of proper names and other words in the LXX Version, as well as, later, in Origen and Jerome. Transliterations of Punic are also found especially in Plautus (Pœnulus Act V). But one of the best means to a knowledge of what Hebrew sounded like as a spoken language, is obtained from hearing modern Arabic. For, as has been said, if Samuel were to rise again from the grave he would be able to make himself understood at the present day. The information to be gained from ancient sources shows that, by the time of the introduction of the punctuation, the language had lost considerably in variety, richness and flexibility of sound. It seems as if the punctuated text were to the living language very much what the mechanical enunciation of Arabic by a European scholar who can pronounce the consonants is to that of an educated Arab.

2. *The Consonants.* As in Arabic, the Hebrew punctuation makes use of a dot to distinguish between two possible phonetic values of the same sign. This is the case with the letters ב ג ד כ פ ת and the letters ה and ש, but the dot placed over the ש to the left or right to distinguish between the sounds *s* and *sh* is, properly speaking, the only diacritical point employed in punctuated Hebrew, in the sense in which one speaks of diacritical points in Arabic. There is no evidence, however, that the use of this point is, as in Arabic, any older than the rest. It was unknown to Jerome and is not heard of any earlier than the others. It is difficult to know what quality of sound was denoted by the letter ש, but it was probably that of the English *s*. The Arabic *sin* has the strong Eastern sound of the Hebrew ס. When it is desired to distinguish between the sounds *s* and *sh* as in Jud. 12, 6 between *sibboleth* and *shibboleth* this is effected by the contrast, not of ש and ש, which could not have been represented in the unpointed text, but by that of ש and ס.

It is not often that a various reading depends on the placing of the diacritical point of this letter, but examples are:—Jer. 5, 7, where MSS. vary between ואשבע, 'and I satisfied them,' which is the better supported reading, and ואשבע, 'and I laid them under an oath,' which is perhaps preferable: Jer. 50, 9 משכיל 'orphan-making' and משכיל, 'well-skilled,' and others. Examples of erroneous pointing are Eccl. 3, 17, where for, 'there is a time there' (שָׁם), we must read 'He has set a time' (שָׂם): Ezek. 39, 26, וְנָשׂוּ for וְנָשְׂאוּ should be וְנָשׁוּ, 'and they shall forget.'

שׁ however was not the only Hebrew character which bore two distinct sounds: it is nearly certain that the ח, and quite certain that the ע, also represent each two phonetic values. ח answers to two Arabic letters ح and خ, the former resembling the Greek χ, the latter the Scotch and German *ch*. ח must also have had these two values and this explains how one root appears to bear so many distinct senses, as חלל=to *profane* حل, and to *be pierced* خل: חרם to *devote* حرم, and to *break through* خرم: חרש to *plough* حرث, and to *be still* خرس. There would be no doubt as to the double value of the ח but for the fact that the versions were unable to transliterate it, especially the Greek versions.

There is no such doubt about ע. This answers to the Arabic ع and غ, the former a peculiarly Semitic sound, the latter *gh* or the Continental *r*. The LXX represent the former by a breathing, that is, omit it, the latter by γ. עזה=Γαζα=Gaza, עמרה=Γομορρα= Gomorrah: עמר=γομορ. On the other hand עמרי=Αμβρι[1]

---

[1] For the β cf. Alhambra=الحمرى and commonly.

= Omri : עזיהו = Οζίας = Uzziah : ישעיהו = Ησαιας = Isaiah.

Further a point was used to distinguish between the hard and soft sounds of ת פ כ ד ג ב, that is between b ב and bh ב and so on. The same point is used in Syriac. In Ginsburg's text the absence of the point is regularly marked by *Raphe*, ב̄ &c. Perhaps it is owing to this double pronunciation that two verses commencing with פ are found in Pss. 25 and 34.[1] The LXX transliterates כ by κ or χ, פ by π or φ, ת by τ or θ. In Baer's edition of the text any letter following a guttural with simple *shevâ* receives this point (Ps. 61, 4 מחסה). Ginsburg condemns this practice as due to misunderstanding the rule describing the word as *dageshed* or 'hardened,' without its being meant that the point should actually be inserted.

3. *Dagesh Forte.* The same point was employed to express the doubling of a consonant. It never seems to have been customary to write a doubled consonant twice. This is done, however, always in the case of the name יששכר LXX Ισσαχαρ and such a form as חצצר is perhaps a double writing of the צ: this seems clearly intended in 2 Chr. 5, 13. Dagesh Forte answers exactly to the Arabic *teshdîd*, but Syriac has no corresponding

---

[1] Yet p is the only one of these twelve sounds which the Arabs cannot make.

point. When D. F. is placed in one of the letters ב ג ד כ פ ת it doubles the hard sound. If it be desired to double the soft sound the letter must be written twice, לבבות *livvôth*. A peculiar feature of pointed Hebrew is that the gutturals and *resh* are not doubled whilst in Arabic any letter whatever may be doubled. This is perhaps owing to the punctuation having been applied so late. There is no reason why these letters should not be doubled, and they are so in the transliterations of the LXX, as חרן=Αρραν: עמרה=Γομορρα: ערבון=άρραβών, the lengthening of the preceding vowel for compensation being dropped. Baer also employs D. F. in the case of a word beginning with the same letter with which the last ended, as Gn. 31, 54 לאכל לחם; but Ginsburg condemns this also.

There are a few remnant cases of gutturals or ר being doubled even in the present text: ויביאו Gen. 43, 26: Ezra 8, 18: cf. Lev. 23, 17, though in these cases the point may equal the Arabic *hamzah* and merely mark the א as a consonant; but there is no doubt about Ezek. 16, 4 כרת שרך: Jer. 39, 12: Job 39, 9 (Baer).

In Arabic as in other languages *n* before *b* is pronounced *m*. Traces of this are Is. 35, 1 יששום: Nu. 3, 49 פדיום: the converse Ezek. 33, 26 עשיתן תועבה.

4. *The Vowels.* Vowel letters are freely used in post-Biblical Hebrew to represent even short vowels. A case

of this in the Old Testament may be Ps. 5, 1 נחילות for חלילים=נחלות. Cf. Is. 33, 1. Before a final guttural there must be an *a* sound, otherwise the guttural cannot be pronounced or can only be pronounced with difficulty, even by an Arab. Hence the *pathah furtive* which is inserted before the final ח, ע and ה when preceded by any long vowel except *a*. To these ק would perhaps have been added in an earlier stage of the language. The punctuators saw the guttural character of ק, for they point it as a guttural in certain cases. But by their time its true sound may have been lost in Hebrew, as it is in many dialects of modern Arabic. Before a guttural *i* and *u* became *e* and *o*. This rule reproduces the sound exactly.

In Syriac *y* before *i* has the sound of א. So it may have been in Hebrew. The LXX transliterate ישראל, Ισραηλ, ישחק Ισαακ but ירמיהו Ιερεμιας. Ben Naphtali is said to have read לישראל, *lisrael* for Ben Asher's *leyisrael*.

The shortest vowel sounds are represented by the *hatephs* and *shevâ*. The last is not used with gutturals, though an exception is ערומים Gen. 2, 25: Some of the oldest MSS. employ *hateph qamets* instead of *kamets hatuph*, as in Baer's text. Baer places *hateph pathah* instead of simple *shevâ* under the first of two identical consonants, e. g. הַלְלוּ. Ginsburg condemns this also.

The *shevâ* would often have no audible sound, as when the following letter was a liquid. Even in Arabic the short vowels are often lost: thus *jawâr* sounds *jwâr*. Neither had *shevâ* a uniform sound: Ben Asher notes the following modifications;—

before *y* it sounds *i* as ביום=*biyom*
before *y* with *i* it sounds *e* as בישראל, *beyisrael*
with *metheg*, e. g. Ps. 51, 2, it sounds *a* as בבוא *babho*
before a guttural it resembles the guttural's sound as מאד, *mo'odh*. Elsewhere it is *e*.

The pausal vowels can hardly have differed in quality from the non-pausal, but only quantitatively. Jeremiah's (22, 29) ארץ ארץ ארץ lose half its force if we say *erets, erets ārets*: cf. Is. 24, 19. This would be avoided by giving long *a* the same thin sound which it has in Arabic in certain positions where it actually is the long of *seghol*.

5. *Summary.* Thus while the punctuation has the appearance of being a merely mechanical classification of vowel sounds, which might be applied to any language, and is applied in the Old Testament to the Aramaic portions as well as to the Hebrew, the system is not so hard and fast as it seems. For, (1) no vowel point had one fixed value but each was modified by the adjacent consonants as in the Arabic *kelb* and *qalb*: (2) the punctuators pointed certain letters, especially the gutturals differently from others and (3) broke through their own rules in order to come closer to the actual sound of the language as known to them. Still whereas in Arabic there are only six vowels, three long and three short, and two diphthongs and these have to be modified according to their consonants, in Hebrew the punctuators made an attempt to express every possible sound by an appropriate sign.

6. *The Accents.* As a further aid towards the correct enunciation of the language and its recitation in public, there were invented two accentual systems, a prose system and a poetical. The former is applied to the prose books and also to portions of the book of Job, as the prologue and epilogue, and the verse introductory of each speaker: the latter, to Psalms, Proverbs and the rest of Job. In the Psalms the titles, whether forming a verse by themselves or only a part of a verse, are joined on to the beginning of the Psalm as if forming a part of it, and similarly such words as סלה are joined to what precedes. This is to be explained by the fact that the accents are in the first place musical notes or combinations of notes, and were designed with a view to the cantillation of the books in the synagogue where the titles were included in the Psalms. But their musical values have been lost.

The accents, in the second place, mark the tone

syllable. But here again it is the tone syllable of the word as sung or recited in public, and the tone is regularly on the last syllable of the word, or, at least, on the second last. But it need not be supposed that this was the place of the tone in ordinary reading or in speaking. In the living language the accent would naturally be retracted towards the beginning of the word as in English and as is practically done in modern spoken Arabic.

But the value of the accents for us lies in their interpunctional power. Music must to some extent conform to the sense, and hence the accents answer to our punctuation and form a sort of running commentary on the text, showing what words were combined together, and which were regarded as being less closely connected. Thus they frequently show in doubtful cases what the opinion of the Massoretes was regarding the connection of the words in a verse. On the other hand the accents frequently show a complete disregard for the sense, as when they join the titles to the beginnings of the Psalms or סלה to the end of the verse in which it occurs.

7. *Peculiar Pointings.* The Massoretes did not always point the text in the most obvious manner, but allowed themselves to be influenced by subjective considerations. The best example of this is the phrase

ראה פני which would naturally be read 'to see the face of.' In Ex. 33, 20, however, it is said 'No man shall see Me and live;' and it is an established doctrine of the Old Testament that the result of seeing God is death: Gn. 32, 31: Jud. 13, 22: Is. 6, 5: an exceptional passage is Ex. 24, 10. Accordingly, when the genitive to the phrase 'to see the face of,' is אלהים or its equivalent, the verb is pointed as a *Niphal* and (את)פני taken—'before', i. e. appear before, e. g. Ps. 42, 3 וְאֵרָאֶה פְּנֵי אלהים where it would have been simpler to read וְאֶרְאֶה. But the Massoretes always do this in this phrase even, e. g. in Dt. 31, 11, Is. 1, 12 reading לְהֵרָאוֹת: i. e. לַרְאוֹת as לראות פני ה' so Dt. 16, 16 יֵרָאֶה כל־זכורך את־פני ה'. It is not certain however whether the Massoretic reading is not the correct one. את־פני does mean 'before' as well as לפני, and the whole phrase is found in 1 S. 1, 22, ונראה את פני ה', 'and he shall appear &c.' though even here perhaps we should read, 'and we shall see &c.' The point is another proof of the reverence with which the consonantal text was regarded.

Other examples of pointings due to dogmatic presuppositions are Eccl. 3, 21, 'Who knoweth the spirit of a man which goeth upward' &c. for 'whether it goeth upward,' הַעֹלָה for הַעֹלֶה: Jer. 34, 18 is untranslatable as it stands because לְפָנַי has been pointed לְפָנָי: it should read 'before the calf': Is. 7, 11 'Ask it in the depth' lit. 'make deep, ask' שַׁאֲלָה, pausal form of emphatic imperative, should be שְׁאָלָה, 'ask it in Sheol.'

Frequently, no doubt the pointing is erroneous. Thus in the phrase 'he was gathered to his peoples' there is no doubt that עַמָּיו is plural, so that עַמִּי should be plural too, 'my peoples,' but it is pointed singular, cf. Gen. 25, 8 and 49, 29.

The punctuators were, however, not themselves responsible for their punctuation. They received what had been handed down to them by oral tradition and what errors there are, date from before their time.

In several places the pointing seems intended to offer a choice of readings as Ps. 7, 6 יִרְדֹּף=יְרַדֵּף or יִרְדָּף: Is. 59, 3 נְגֹאֲלוּ niphal or pual and frequently.

CHAPTER XI.

THE MASSORAH.

1. *Definition of the Term.* The word Massorah (מָסוֹרָה or מְסוֹרָה) or, as it is more properly written in the Mishnah, Massoreth (מָסוֹרֶת) is derived from the root מסר, Nu. 31, 5 (16), signifying 'to hand down,' *tradere*, and means what is handed down, in this case the traditional text of Scripture. The Massorah as a whole had its beginnings in very early times. R. Aqiba (†

c. 135) called it a 'hedge about the Law' (Aboth III, 13: מָסוֹרֶת סְיָג לַתּוֹרָה).¹ The textual Massorah has been described as 'a mass of grammatical, lexicographical and concordantial notices' concerning the text. It gives the result one would get by turning up Fürst's or Buxtorf's Concordance and noting the number of times a particular expression occurs. It mentions synonymous expressions; but very rarely attempts to distinguish between the different senses in which any given expression is used, as it does in the case of the word כָּאֲרִי which occurs only in Ps. 22, 17 and Is. 38, 13. The Massorah on the latter passage remarks that כארי is used in different senses in the two passages. It has been compared in some of its parts to Alford's Greek Testament, if there, instead of chapter and verse, a few words of the context were cited. Each copyist or teacher made notes in the course of his work and these were preserved so that the Massorah represents the result of the labours of generations of scholars. Otherwise the work could never have been accomplished, as it was accomplished, without the aid of grammar, lexicon or concordance.

In the Massorah are distinguished the *M. parva*, the *M. magna* and the *M. finalis*, according to the place

---

¹ מסרת Ezek. 20, 37 is for מאסרת.

occupied on the codex with reference to the text. The M. parva consists of brief and detached remarks generally expressed by a single letter, giving the number of occurrences, which are placed in the side margin of the columns. These notes were afterwards collected and classified, and lists of them appended in the top and bottom margins, above and below the text in which one of them occurred: this is the M. magna. Those lists which were too long for insertion on the page were either prefixed at the beginning or added at the end of MSS., generally at the end, whence they are called (inaccurately) the M. finalis. It is pretty much a distinction without a difference.

It has to be borne in mind that the Massorah is not one but many. As there was an Eastern and a Western recension of the text, so there was an Eastern and a Western Massorah. And as every standard codex varied in some slight details from the other, so the lists of occurrences of particular expressions based upon it would vary from other lists or rubrics based upon other codices. Hence the Massorah as a whole is frequently in conflict with itself. The whole of the Massorah magna or parva on any passage is never found in any one MS. but some in one and some in another. To obtain the whole of it it is necessary to collate all known MSS.

2. *The Qrîs and Sevîrs.* One of the main features of the Massorah is its preservation of the *qrîs*. This is the only part of it which is found as a whole in all printed texts and codices. All printed texts are supposed to show all the *qrîs*. In the Massorah itself the *qrîs* are found in three forms. 1. Each *qrî* is given in the margin opposite to its *Kthîbh* in the text, a small circle or asterisk (which has no name) being placed over the word in the text to draw attention to the margin. 2. Those *qrîs* occurring in any book were collected together and added at the end of the book. 3. The whole of the *qrîs* were collected from the whole text and arranged in lists or rubrics according to the root or particle or letter in question.

To what extent the *qrîs* are based upon MS. authority, and so represent true various readings, it is impossible to determine. Many of them are no doubt mere corrections of the text, generally wrong, where it was supposed to be corrupt. There is a certain class of *qrîs* which profess to be nothing more than such conjectural emendations of the text, but which there is reason to believe are genuine various readings. These are the *qrîs* called סבירין, plural of the pass. pc. of סבר to opine, think. What one MS. denotes as a סביר is in another designated a קרי and vicê versâ, so that the terms seem to be interchangeable. One peculiarity is said to be that the סביר represents the Eastern text reading, and the versions frequently agree with them as against the Western text, pointing to their being true various readings. Thus in Gn. 49, 13 על צידון the סביר is עד which most versions read. Perhaps just because the סברין represent various readings, they were neglected by the later redactors who looked upon the text as fixed. They were unofficial *qrî* not found in the official lists, and so disregarded. And they have met the same fate at the hands of modern Editors. Hahn's Text, Leipsic 1893, is said to mention only two; 1 S. 2, 16 לא for לו (Baer has קרי לא) and 12, 5 ויאמרו for ויאמר, which Baer omits altogether, as also Gn. 49, 13 above. In fact Baer never gives the סביר in the margin of the text but only in the notes at the end. Jacob ben Chaiyim, Bomberg's editor, knew about two hundred, and Ginsburg has collected a hundred and fifty more. But the whole subject has been much neglected.

The majority of the *qrîs* are undoubtedly mere emendations of the text answering to the *errata* and *corrigenda* of a modern printed book, only with the disadvantage of not having been placed there by the author. Such are the four *qri perpetua*, יהוה, הוא, ירושלם, יששכר which have no corresponding marginal note in present texts. Frequently the Kthîbh represents an archaic form which the Massoretes did not recognise, such as מלוכי Jud. 9, 10 (Baer): Is. 32, 11 (rightly pointed): Jud. 9, 8. These are not exclusively pausal forms. Sometimes the *qrîs* are indubitably correct as Amos 8, 8 נשקה, *qrî* נשקעה as 9, 5. In the Venice Bible of 1521, the word for 'sheep' 1 S. 17, 34, שה, was misprinted זו. Instead of correcting the text a *qrî* שה was put in the margin and remained there until very recently, later editors having copied it in turn. There is no such *qrî*: all codices and earliest printed texts have שה.

The *qrîs* are much older than the Massoretes, who only put down in black and white what had been handed down to them from previous ages. They show an early stage of textual criticism, when subjective and doctrinal considerations were taken account of in altering the reading of the text, and MSS. varying from the received text were sparingly taken advantage of. Sometimes copyists inserted the *qrî* in the text but the regular course was to leave what was considered to be the wrong reading in the text and relegate the supposed correct reading to the margin. For the Massoretes were not collating many MSS. but stedfastly and faithfully following one.

3. *Other Parts of the Massorah*. In the margin alongside of the *qrîs* attention is drawn to the manner

in which a word is written, as with a redundant vowel-letter, or defectively, or in any peculiar way: or whether the vowel is prolonged in pause or not. The technical terms are pointed and translated at the end of printed texts: in Baer's text at the end of each book separately. Occasional attempts were made to explain the form, sometimes rather far-fetched, as Gen. 1, 21 תנינם, the י has no mate because leviathan has none: Gen. 2, 7, וייצר is written *plene* because this was the fulfilling of the creation; otherwise it is ויצר. Cf. v. 19.

A direction for the arrangement of the text on the page is found Gen. 49, 8: Dt. 31, 28 and elsewhere.

At the conclusion of each book is a note of the number of sections, open and shut, verses, *qrî* and so on, contained in it. In most texts the Christian chapters[1] are given also but this is, of course, an innovation of Christian printers. It was begun by Athias in 1659—61. The note is introduced by the word חזק, 'Be strong' (2 S. 10, 12).

The last verses of Is., Mal., Lam., and Eccl. are followed by a repetition of the last but one, from a dislike to ending with ill-omened words. The sign is יתקק i. e. קהלת, קינה, תרי עשר, ישעיה.

The Law was usually copied by professional scribes,

---

[1] Called פרקים.

the other books by ordinary teachers and readers, whose object was to copy as much as possible in a given time and so earn more. They are mentioned among those for whom Gehenna is prepared, but some were very faithful scribes.

CHAPTER XII.

MANUSCRIPTS AND PRINTED TEXTS.

1. *Manuscripts.* The oldest dated MS. of any part of the O. T. is the St. Petersburg Codex of the Prophets, of 916, and it is generally believed to be the oldest of any, though Ginsburg believes a Brit. Mus. MS. of the Pentateuch (Orient. 4445) to be "at least half a century earlier." The latter consists of 186 folios, 55 of which, however, have been added by a later hand, and are dated 1540 A.D. Each page contains three columns generally of 21 lines each. The lines are unequal as the dilatable letters (אהלתם) had not yet come into use. The Massorah magna has been added by a later hand in the upper and lower margins, generally two lines at the top and four at the foot of the page, and the Massorah parva by the same hand, in the side margins and between the columns. The punctuation and accentuation are on the Palestinian

[To face p. 126]

PAGE OF HEBREW MS.

A PAGE OF HEBREW MS. OF ABOUT THE BEGINNING OF THE 10th CENTURY, A.D.
(BRITISH MUSEUM, OR. 4445.)

Exodus xix. 24—xx. 17, with the Massorah Magna and Parva.

System, whereas those of the St. Petersburg Codex are on the Babylonian. It shows a few variations from the textus receptus, *viz.*;—

(1) In the division of the text into open and closed sections, it departs from the received text in 116 instances. The annual pericopes coincide with those of the received text. They are separated by a vacant space and the word פרש is put in the margin opposite. The triennial pericopes or 154 סדרים are indicated in a list at the end.

(2) Originally there was no verse-division beyond marking the last word of each verse with *silluq*, but a later hand has inserted *soph pasuq*.

(3) Some of the consonants are peculiarly formed. The left limb of the ה is joined to the top bar as in the ח. They are distinguished by the crossbar of the ח projecting a little to the left. The י approaches the form of ו in length. The final *nun* ן is, on the other hand, short and hardly distinguishable from a ז.

(4) The *Beghadhkephath* letters when without *dagesh*, and ה when without *mappik*, are generally marked with *raphe*.

(5) *Qamets* is a horizontal bar with a dot below— its primitive form.

(6) *Metheg* is very rarely and irregularly used, being omitted even before vocal shevâ.

The St. Petersburg Codex of 916 A. D., consisting of about 225 folios, each of two columns of 21 lines, is the oldest dated Hebrew MS. It contains the latter prophets: Is., Jer., Ezek., and the XII. It generally has two lines of the Massora magna in the bottom margin and the Massora parva between the columns. It has the same peculiar י ה and final ן as the preceding; but it has already the *soph pasuq* between the verses. But the distinguishing feature of this MS. is that it exhibits the superlinear or Babylonian system of punctuation. In the lists at the end, the order of the books varies: even Is. Jer. and Ezek. having no fixed sequence.

Most MSS. contain only the Law or the Prophets or the Hagiographa. The oldest MS. of the whole of the Old Testament is, like the last, one of the Firkowitzsch collection, and belongs to the year 1010 A. D. But Wickes disputes the date.

The MSS. of the Massoretic Text contain various readings like any other MSS., though the M. T. itself can scarcely be said to have various readings. Instances of variations which are not mere scribal errors and which affect the consonants are such as e. g. the prep. כ for ב as in Is. 2, 6 בילדי '(they make agreements) with or like the children (of strangers)': Ps. 102, 4 'My days are consumed in smoke or like smoke': Jer. 18, 4

Jes. 14,31 – 16,?

נָמוֹג פְּלֶשֶׁת כֻּלֵּךְ כִּי מִצָּפוֹן
עָשָׁן בָּא וְאֵין בּוֹדֵד
בְּמוֹעָדָיו וּמַה־יַּעֲנֶה
מַלְאֲכֵי־גוֹי כִּי יְהוָה יִסַּד
צִיּוֹן וּבָהּ יֶחֱסוּ עֲנִיֵּי עַמּוֹ
מַשָּׂא מוֹאָב
כִּי בְּלֵיל שֻׁדַּד עָר מוֹאָב
נִדְמָה כִּי בְּלֵיל שֻׁדַּד קִיר
מוֹאָב נִדְמָה עָלָה הַבַּיִת
וְדִיבֹן הַבָּמוֹת לְבֶכִי עַל
נְבוֹ וְעַל מֵידְבָא מוֹאָב
יְיֵלִיל בְּכָל־רֹאשָׁיו קָרְחָה
וְכָל־זָקָן גְּרוּעָה בְּחוּצֹתָיו
חָגְרוּ שָׂק עַל־גַּגּוֹתֶיהָ
וּבִרְחֹבֹתֶיהָ כֻּלֹּה יְיֵלִיל
יָרַד בַּבֶּכִי וַתִּזְעַק חֶשְׁבּוֹן
וְאֶלְעָלֵה עַד־יַהַץ נִשְׁמַע
קוֹלָם עַל־כֵּן חֲלֻצֵי מוֹאָב
יָרִיעוּ נַפְשׁוֹ יָרְעָה לּוֹ
לִבִּי לְמוֹאָב יִזְעָק בְּרִיחֶיהָ
עַד־צֹעַר עֶגְלַת שְׁלִשִׁיָּה

כִּי מַעֲלֵה הַלּוּחִית בִּבְכִי
יַעֲלֶה־בּוֹ כִּי דֶּרֶךְ חוֹרֹנַיִם
זַעֲקַת־שֶׁבֶר יְעֹעֵרוּ כִּי־מֵי
נִמְרִים מְשַׁמּוֹת יִהְיוּ כִּי־
יָבֵשׁ חָצִיר כָּלָה דֶשֶׁא
יֶרֶק לֹא הָיָה עַל־כֵּן יִתְרָה
עָשָׂה וּפְקֻדָּתָם עַל נַחַל
הָעֲרָבִים יִשָּׂאוּם כִּי־הִ
קִּיפָה הַזְּעָקָה אֶת־
גְּבוּל מוֹאָב עַד־אֶגְלַיִם
יִלְלָתָהּ וּבְאֵר אֵילִים
יִלְלָתָהּ כִּי מֵי דִימוֹן מָלְאוּ
דָם כִּי־אָשִׁית עַל־דִּימוֹן
נוֹסָפוֹת לִפְלֵיטַת מוֹאָב
אַרְיֵה וְלִשְׁאֵרִית אֲדָמָה
שִׁלְחוּ־כַר מֹשֵׁל־אֶרֶץ
מִסֶּלַע מִדְבָּרָה אֶל־הַר
בַּת־צִיּוֹן וְהָיָה כְעוֹף־נוֹדֵד
קֵן מְשֻׁלָּח תִּהְיֶינָה בְּנוֹת
מוֹאָב מַעְבָּרֹת לְאַרְנוֹן
הָבִיאוּ עֵצָה עֲשׂוּ פְלִילָה

THE ST. PETERSBURG CODEX.

'in clay' and 'as clay': but practically they are confined to the pointing.

But the majority of various readings are mere scribal errors, chiefly omissions, arising from homœoteleuton. Thus, one MS. omits nine words in Gn. 19, 20, and in Ex. 8 omits vv. 10 and 11, another omits ten words in Gn. 31, 52 (from 'this heap' to 'this heap'), with many other omissions and insertions. In 1 Chr. 11 one MS. has twenty-two variations from the MT. including four omissions from homœoteleuton, another has seventeen, another thirteen and another twenty-eight. The number of omissions from homœoteleuton makes it probable that there are such in the MT. itself. Errors due to mistaking one letter for another of similar form are more frequent in Hebrew MSS. than in Latin or Greek.

2. *Printed Editions.* The earliest editions of the printed text were, naturally, the work of Jewish hands.

I. The first portion of the Old Testament to be printed was the Psalter which appeared in the year 1477, at what place is unknown. The text is printed in Hebrew with the commentary of Kimchi in Rabbinic. Text and commentary alternate generally at every verse. The end of a verse is marked by *soph pasuq*. The first few Psalms are vowelled; but the difficulty seems to have been too great, and the pointing is discontinued, vowel-letters being used instead, as in later Hebrew. The text displays many errors, words and even verses being omitted, and letters and words repeated. The Massoretic *qrîs* are mostly read in the text. Copies of this Psalter are rare: one is in the British Museum. It was twice re-issued 1478—80.

II. In 1482 the first edition of the Pentateuch was printed with points at Bologna, and possibly the Five Rolls at the same time. The former was accompanied by the Targum of Onkelos and the commentary of Rashi.

III. In 1485-6 the first (unpointed) edition of the Prophets, former and later, was printed at Soncino in Lombardy, with the commentaries of Rashi and Kimchi.

IV. In 1486-7 the Hagiographa was printed (with vowel points but not accents), with commentaries, at Naples. In nos. III and IV יהוה and אלהים are spelled יהדה and אלדים.

V. The second edition of the Pentateuch, printed at Faro in Portugal in 1487, is the first text printed without a commentary: it has vowels but no accents.

VI. The Editio Princeps of the whole Old Testament, with points and accents but no commentary, was finished at Soncino, 14th February 1488. The whole text was printed a second time at Naples 1491-3; and a third time in the Brescia Bible of 1494.

The last is interesting as having been the text used by Luther.

These Six Editions were all those published up to that date. There was no further issue of a text for sixteen years, owing to the distress resulting from the persecution of the Jews, and their expulsion from Spain in 1492. The fourth edition of the whole of the Old Testament was printed at Pesaro in 1511-17.

The first Christian edition of the Hebrew Text is that contained in the Complutensian Polyglot, published under the inspiration of Cardinal Ximenes who adopted the idea from Origen, printed at the University founded by him at Alcala, 'quae dicitur esse Complutum; sit vel ne, nil mihi curae,' says Peter Martyr. In the Old Testament the Hebrew Text is accompanied by the LXX, Vulgate or Jerome, in three columns on one page, the Hebrew and Greek being placed on either side of the Vulgate, 'duos hinc et inde latrones, medium autem Jesum, hoc est, Romanam sive Latinam ecclesiam collocantes.' Ximenes allowed the pre-eminent value of the Hebrew. The Targum of Onkelos is also inserted.

Before commencing this great undertaking, Ximenes had to cast all his own types. Hence the defective character of the pointing, which seems to have been always running short of *hatephs*, so that these had to be represented by short vowels. The accentuation is confined to *athnah*, with *soph pasuq*. *Maqqeph* is not used nor are the dilatable letters, short lines being filled up with *yods*. *Mehuppach* is used to mark servile letters so as to guide readers to the root. Every Hebrew word is lettered and there is a corresponding letter on its Latin equivalent. As a further aid the roots of words are placed in the margin. The verses were not yet numbered, but otherwise the text is divided and arranged after the model of the Vulgate; thus for the first time discarding the Massoretic sections in favour of the Christian chapters. The following will give some idea of the immense difficulties with which Ximenes had to contend: only the irregular punctuation is given.

ⁿעֲשֹׂה | לַעֲשׂוֹת ᵐלִשְׁמֹר ˡמְאֹד ᵏוְאָמֵץ ⁱחֲזַק ʰרַק
יְצַוָּה ⁱיָרָה | עַבְדִּי ʰמֹשֶׁה ᵍצִוָּה ᶠאֲשֶׁר ᵉוַיַּעֲבֹר ᵈהַתּוֹרָה ᶜכָּל

This labour of fifteen years was finished on 10th July 1517: Ximenes died on 8th November of the same year, at the age of 81.

The value of this monument of human skill and perseverance is practically nothing. The Hebrew did not present a new text and, if it had, its value would have lain in the pointing, which here is most defective. In the LXX there is no doubt that at least a few liturgical passages were forced into conformity with the Vulgate.

RABBINIC BIBLE (Jud. 5, 12—16).

Nor do the MSS. on which these texts were based seem to have been of any great antiquity; for in the year 1749 they were sold to a person who manufactured rockets, which would indicate that they were made of paper.

The first Rabbinic Bible, that is, the text with all the points, the Massorahs, Targums, Midrashim and the commentaries of the Rabbis was printed by Daniel Bomberg at Venice in 1516-17. The division of Samuel, Kings and Chronicles, each into two books, and of Ezra into Ezra and Nehemiah, is first *marked* here in a purely Hebrew Text, and for the first time the consonants of the *qrîs* are given in the margin. Before this only the points were inserted in the text, and the reader had to find the consonants for himself. Thus in Is. 44, 14 Luther, who used the Brescia Bible, naturally did not observe the small ן, taking it for a ו and translating accordingly. The edition of 1516-17 also gives many various readings affecting the consonants, if not the sense. This Bible however appealed neither to Jews (being edited by a Christian, Felix Pratensis), nor to the Christians, who could not read the Rabbinic commentaries.

What is called the 'editio princeps' of the Rabbinic Bible with Massorah is Bomberg's second edition, and the first edited by Jacob ben Chaiyim, a Jew of Tunis,

1524-5. This forms the standard edition of the Massoretic Text.

This edition departs from ancient rule [1] and distinguishes open and closed sections by inserting the letters פ and ס, and closing the line in both cases. Samuel and Kings are treated as two books each, for the first time, but in the Massoretic summary given at the ends of the books they are each treated as one. In the arrangement of the page the Hebrew and Aramaic form the two central columns, with the Massorah magna above and below and the Massorah parva between, whilst all around lie two commentaries. The lists too long for insertion on the page are given at the end of Chronicles.

This is the only authorised Massoretic recension, which may not be departed from without good authority. Ginsburg notes the following points: (1) the consonants of the *qrîs* given in the margin are now first marked with ק, thus distinguishing them from various readings; (2) it first takes account of the סבירין; (3) it also shows various readings from MSS. outside of the Massorah. Jacob b. Chaiyim was able to collect only a comparatively small part of the existing Massorah, so that subsequent editors may have good authority for departing from his readings.

---

[1] See p. 96 note.

Another edition printed by Bomberg was published 1525-8. It followed partly Felix Pratensis and partly J. b. Chaiyim. It was much used by the Reformers, and Ginsburg's copy is said to have notes in the handwriting of Luther.

The Biblia Sacra of Arias Montanus 1567-71 is a polyglot. The Hebrew is accompanied by Aramaic and Greek with Latin translations of all three. It is beautifully printed in large clear type, widely spaced, with the dilatable letters, and the numbers of the chapters are indicated by Hebrew letters inserted for the first time in the text, the verses being numbered at the side margin. The Massoretic sections are not rigidly observed nor the פ and ס of Jacob ben Chaiyim used. Every page begins and ends with the beginning or end of a sentence. There are no *qrîs* or other notes on the page.

Buxtorf's Rabbinic Bible appeared 1618-19.

The Paris Polyglot by Le Jay was published 1629-44.

In emulation of the last there appeared 1654-57 the London Polyglot, generally known as Brian Walton's. He was an English clergyman who was deprived of his benefices in 1641, having made himself obnoxious to the Puritan party. The work owes its existence however to the generosity of the government of Cromwell to whom it was originally dedicated, though this dedication was on, the Restoration, torn out and one to Charles II substituted. This was the second work published by subscription in England, the price being £10. It is in six volumes folio, and is notable as giving the Ethiopic and Persian Versions for the first time. The Aramaic paraphrases are also very complete. It has, besides the Vulgate, Latin translations of the Hebrew, LXX, Syriac, Targum, Samaritan and Arabic, so far as they go. There are no Massoretic notes on the page.

The edition of Athias 1661 first inserted the Christian chapters in the Massoretic Summary at the end of the books, but only in the case of the Law.

1705. Van der Hooght, often re-edited.

1744. The Mantua edition inserted the number of chapters in the summaries to all the books: in it is embodied the Massoretic commentary of Solomon de Norzi (1626).

The Editions which make the widest use of the Massorah are those of Baer and Ginsburg. The former wants Ex.—Deut.: Baer unfortunately died in 1897.

3. *The Chapters.* In modern editions the Hebrew Text is divided into chapters which correspond very nearly to those found in the English Version, each chapter being divided into verses which are numbered

in the margin. These chapters had their origin in the Vulgate and have been variously ascribed to Lanfranc, archbishop of Canterbury, † 1089: Stephen Langton, † 1228; and, with most probability, to Hugo de Sancto Caro in the thirteenth century. There should, however, properly be no such breaks as these on the Hebrew page, except where the Massoretic sections coincide with the Christian chapters, as in the majority of cases they do. The first Jew known to have made use of the latter division is R. Solomon ben Israel about A.D. 1330. His motive was to facilitate reference for the purposes of controversy. He placed the numbers of the chapters in the margin, and they were sometimes so inscribed on ancient codices by their owners or by later scribes. But until 1517 there were no breaks in printed texts other than the Massoretic sections. It was in the polyglot Bibles, in which the Greek and Latin Versions were printed alongside of the Hebrew, that these were first discarded in favour of the Christian chapters. This was first done in the Complutensian Polyglot. The numbers of the chapters were still, however, confined to the margin. The first to break up and insert the numbers into the body of the text seems to have been Arias Montanus in his edition with interlinear Latin translation, Antwerp 1571. The first edition of the Hebrew text by itself in which the text was thus broken up was that of 1573-4 (printed like the last by Plantin) and the practice was adopted even by Jewish Editors. Modern editions mark the verse-numbers in the margin in Arabic numerals, except the fives which are indicated by the Hebrew letters ה, י and so on, only 15 is denoted by טו instead of יה because the latter are the first two letters of the name יהוה.

4. *Clausulae Massoreticae.* One example of the colophon at the end of a book may serve for all. That to the Psalms in the edition of Van der Hooght published by Judah d'Allemand in 1822 runs as follows:—

חזק

סכום פסוקי דספר תהלים אלפים וחמש מאות ועשרים ושבעה· וסימנו אהבתי מעון ביתך ומקום משכן כבודך· וחציו ויפתוהו בפיהם· וסדריו תשעה עשר· וסימנו המשביע בטוב עדיך:

"Be strong!" The number of the verses of the Book of Psalms is 2527; and its sign is Ps. 26, 8 $[1+2+400+10+70+6+700+2+10+400+500+100+6+300+20=2527]$; and its middle [verse] Ps. 78, 36; and its *sidars*, 19; and their sign Ps. 103, 5 $[2+9+6+2=19]$.

Instead of the simple חזק found at the end of individual books, some editions give a more extended formula at the close of the whole Bible and elsewhere, such as;—

חזק ונתחזק המחוקק לא יוזק

The two letters following, kindly supplied by Professor Robertson, give some of the interpretations put upon these words:—

I.

Friday, 29th Nov. 1872.

Dear Dr. Riggs,

My Jew gives a simple enough explanation of the formula at the end of the Hebrew Bible. Whether it is correct or not you must judge for yourself, but he gives it with great confidence.

At the end of the reading of a book of the Law in the synagogue, it is the custom for the Hazzan to say to the person who has just read (any members of the synagogue may be called to read if they are able), חזק *=be strong=well done. The congregation responds* חזק ונתחזק, *"be strong, be strong and we shall strengthen ourselves."*

At the end of the whole Bible the formula is expanded by the addition of the words you pointed out, the meaning of which my Rabbi says is simply this: 'and the printer (lit. engraver) will receive no damage;' יוזק being thus Hoph. of נזק, the verb which gives its name to the Talmudic treatise נזיקין, the mater lectionis being used to indicate the want of the qibbuts, as so often in late Hebrew—

Does it satisfy you?

yours very sincerely

Jas. Robertson.

II.

Constantinople, April 2, 1873.

Rev. Jas. Robertson.

My Dear Brother,

It is curious what a variety of interpretations can be put upon the words at the close of the Hebrew Bible.

Dr. Eppstein of Smyrna read the word המחוקק *as a passive and interpreted it as meaning the* **person instructed in the law.** *Respecting* יוזק *he was in doubt.*

Mr. Reichhardt of Alexandria also regards המחוקק

as a passive; but interprets it to mean the revised text of the Scripture. He regards יוקק as fut. Hoph. of זקק and confidently says that the whole phrase "simply states that the editor has thoroughly revised the Hebrew text so that it would not allow of any more corrections." This he wrote after seeing what you kindly wrote me, and after hearing of Dr. Eppstein's interpretation.

I feel better satisfied with your Rabbi's interpretation than with either of the others. Buxtorf gives to מחוקק in Rabbinic, the meaning printer.

I remain
   My dear Sir
      Most truly yours
         Elias Riggs.

INDEX OF SCRIPTURE TEXTS.

(The references are to the pages, and the order of the books is that of the Hebrew Bible).

Genesis

1	1	pages 36. 65
	21	125
2	4	65
	7, 19	125
	12	52
	25	114
4	7	103
6	9	95
12	18	95
14	2	52
16	5	56
18	5	80
	9	57
	21	38
	22	76
19	33, 35	57, 58
23	2	65
24	7	38
	55	80
25	8	119
27	46	65
	11	43
30	28	90
	32	54
	42	65
31	52	129
32	31	118
33	4	58
35	2	86
36	27	31

Genesis

37	2, 12	59
43	26	113
45	14, 15	58
47	28	96
48	7	39
49	8	125
	10	75
	13 (*bis*)	123
	19, 20	44
	29	119

Exodus

4	2	43
6	28	96
15	1—19	97
17	4	4
20	2	72
21	8	86
22	27	75
23	19	65
24	7	4, 22
	10	118
27	10	23
30	6	83
32	15	49
	25	65
33	20	118
34	7, 14	65
	26	65

Leviticus

1	1	65
6	2	65
8	7	92
10	16	92
11	14	32, 86
	21	86
	30	65
	42	65, 66, 92
13	33	65
20	10	83
23	17	113
24	11	90
25	30	86

Numbers

3	39	55, 59
	49	113
9	10	55, 56, 60
10	35, 36	63, 64
11	15	76
12	12	76
13	30	65
14	17	65
21	14	4, 37
	30	60
24	22, 24	26
25	11	65
	12	67
26	8	86
	35	32
27	5	65
28	13	61
29	15	61
31	2	80
	5, 16	119
	24	65

Deuteronomy

6	4	65
14	13	32, 86
16	16	118
18	13	65
27	4	29
28	30	91

Deuteronomy

29	22	39
	27	65
	28	61
31	11	118
	27	65
	28	125
32	1—43	97
	4, 6	65
	10	78
	13	52, 93
	18	65
33	2	43

Joshua

6	13	84, 92
9	4	85
10	13	37
12	9—24	97
13	26	92
21		31
	32	32, 52
	36, 37 (A. v.)	83
22	34	83
24	27	83

Judges

Ch. 5		97
5	14	5
6	32	74
8	14	5
	35 (*bis*)	74
9	8, 10	124
	27	75
10	8	92
12	6	110
13	22	118
16	25	43
18	30	66
19	18	68
20	13	91

I Samuel

1	1	48
	22	118
2	3	86

INDEX OF SCRIPTURE TEXTS.

1 Samuel

2	16	86, 123
3	13	77
6	11	91
8	2	86
9	1	43
10	25	6
12	5	123
13	1	87
14	50, 51	84
16	11	59
17	34	124
20	2	86
	40	48
24	9	43
25	22	75
28	24	92, 98
31	3	82

2 Samuel

1	6	82
	18	37, 82
Ch.	2—4	73
3	7	87
4	4	74
5	2	43
	16	74
6	3, 4	83
7	12, 14	75
8	3	91
	17	6
10	12	125
	18	69
11	14	6
	21	74
12	14	75
13	33	91
	37	85
15	21	91
16	12	77
	18	86
	23	91
17	3	84
	28	83
18	20	91

2 Samuel

19	20	63
20	1	78
21	19	83
Ch.	22	97
22	7	86
	11 (*bis*)	32
	12	32
Ch.	23	31
23	8	83
	18, 19	87
	29	32
	35	32
24	1	75
	13	69

1 Kings

5	6	69
6	2	85
	8	83
7	41	31
8	48	53
	53	37
12	16	78
	18	86
17	15	52
21	10	74
22	6	92

2 Kings

1	1 & ch. 3	8
5	7	25
	18	91
8	10	86
	26	69
11	1	86
14	6	84
16	6	85
17	24	27, 29
18	20	53
	26	25
	27	91
19	31, 37	91
20	6—8	85
	20	9
22	19	72

Isaiah

1	12	94, 118
2	6	128
3	8	93
	15	43
	23	21
6	5	118
7	11	119
8	1	21 (*bis*), 24, 25
	6	9
	12	84
	21	75
9	2	86
	6	43, 50
15 and 16		8
18	2	22
21	11	39
	16	87
24	19	115
	23	103
26	14	103
30	8	22
	33	52
32	11	124
33	21	92
34	4	41
35	1	113
36	5	53
	11	25
38	13	120
	21, 22	85
40	31	83
41	1	83
44	9	63
	14	66, 133
	24	43
49	5	86
52	8	49
53	7	83
56	9	96
	10	65
59	3	119
63	9	86
66	24	125

Jeremiah

2	11	78
3	19	68
	24	73
5	7	110
	25	92
6	7	92
	11	68
	29	43
9	5, 6	45
	7	84
14	2	66
15	10	82
17	1	21
18	3	43
	4	128
21	1, 3	86
22	14	82
	29	115
23	33	47
25	26	11
	37	68
27	1	86
31	38	91
	40	85
34	18	118
35	11	27
36	18	21
	23	22
38	16	91
39	12	91, 113
	13	66
44	18	43
Ch. 48		8
50	9	110
	29	91
51	1	11
	3	91
	39	78
	41	11

Ezekiel

2	9	22
8	6	43
	17	78

INDEX OF SCRIPTURE TEXTS.

9	2	21
16	4	113
20	37	120
32	29	51
33	26	113
39	26	111
41	20	63
42	9	43
43	13	87
46	22	63
48	16	91

Hosea

1	2	94
2	18	73
4	6	52
	7	79
	11	94
6	5	48
8	12	6, 52
9	10	73
	16	52
10	14	92
11	2	44
12	12	51

Joel

1	12	43

Amos

2	13	79
6	12	81
8	8: 9, 5	124
9	12	51

Micah

1	15	93
3	2	52, 92
	12	98

Nahum

1	3	66
	12	48

Habakkuk

1	12	78
2	1	49

Haggai

1	15	96

Zechariah

2	12	78
9	12	23
11	11	48

Malachi

1	13	78
3	22	65
	24	125

Psalms

1		45
5	1	114
	5	68
7	6	119
9	and 10	12, 45
10	10	43
14		72
16	3	48
	10	93
18	7	86
	11, 12	32
22	17	120
25	and 34	12, 112
27	5	66
	13	61, 64
31	3	32
	7	67
35	7	85
36	7	80
37		12
40	8, 9	82
	14—18	72
42	and 43	45
42	3	118
	6, 7, 12	44
43	5	44
44	5	48
45	2	21
50	7	72
51	2	115
53		72

Psalms

55	16	43
61	4	112
65	8	97
68	26	80
70		72
71	3	32
73	2	84
	4	44
	16	53
80	14	66
	16	65
84	4	65
90	2, 11	45, 97
100	3	86
102	4	128
106	7	44
	20	79
	47, 48	98, 99
107	23—28, 40	64
108		72
110	3	85
111		12
112		12
114	and 115	45
116		45
119		12
123	4	43
130	3	100
139	16	86
140	13	53
142	4	79
143	4	79
144		72
145		12
147		45

Proverbs

1	1	65
2	20	67
10	10	83
11	16	83
13	19	67
16	13	67
	28	66
19	7	86
19	19	85
26	2	86
28	17	66
30	15	66
31	10—30	12

Job

1	5: 2, 5, 9	74
7	5	66
	20	79
9	34	65
10	22	96
13	15	86
16	14	66
19	24	20, 21
23	12	84
27	18	84
31	11	52
32	3	79
33	9	66
38	1	43, 50
	12	43
	13, 15	66
39	9	113
40	6	43, 50
41	4	86

Song of Songs

1	1	65

Ruth

3	3	65
	5, 12, 17	91

Lamentations

1	—4	12
1	6	43
	12: 2 9	66
3	20	79
	36	66
4	3	43
	14	66
5	22	125

Ecclesiastes

3	17	111
	21	118
5	8	53
7	1: 12 13	65
12	14	125

Esther

1	6	65
8	9	23, 30
9	6, 29	65
	7, 9	66
	6—10	97

Daniel

6	20	65, 66

Ezra

Ch. 2		69
2	2	32
4	2	86
	7	26
	12	43
8	18	113

Nehemiah

2	13	43, 50
Ch. 7		69
7	7	32
8	8	93
10	21	18
11	17	31
12	3 & 15	31
13	28	29

1 Chronicles

1	1	65
	42	31
3	8	74
	22	86
5	18	43

1 Chronicles

Ch. 6		31
6	13	86
	61	32, 52
	78, 79	83
7	20	32
8	29—38	83
	33	73
	34	74
9	4	43
	35—44	83
	39	73
Ch. 11		31
11	11	83
	20	86
	30, 37	32
14	7	74
16	35, 36	98
17	10	44
	11, 13	75
19	18	69
20	5	83
21	1	75
	12	69
24	15	18
27	12	43, 50

2 Chronicles

3	4	85
4	11, 16	31
5	13	112
9	25	69
10	16	78
	18	86
12	16	78
21	20: 22, 2	69
22	6	87
	10	86
32	30	9
34	6	43
	27	72

PRINTED BY W. DRUGULIN, LEIPZIG (GERMANY).

www.ingramcontent.com/pod-product-compliance
Lightning Source LLC
Chambersburg PA
CBHW031439160426
43195CB00010BB/791